VOCABULARY

FOR THE

COLLEGE BOUND

BOOK ORANGE

PRESTWICK HOUSE, INC.
"Everything for the English Classroom!"

P. O. Box 246
Cheswold, DE 19936
1.800.932.4593
www.prestwickhouse.com

© Copyright 1999 All rights reserved.
No portion may be reproduced without
permission in writing from the publisher.
Revised June, 2002

ISBN 1-58049-258-4

Strategies for Completing Activities

Analogies ///

While analogies can be a bit confusing when first seen, analogies can be viewed as challenging mind games once the logic of the question is understood. Here is the strategy we recommend.

1. Change the symbols into words.
    Pistol : Weapon :: Rose :
    A pistol is to a weapon as a rose is to a _____

2. Determine the relationship in the first set and put it in a sentence.
    A pistol is one kind of a weapon.

3. Complete the second part.
    A pistol is one kind of a weapon; therefore, a rose is one kind of flower.

    Analogies can be of many different types, but the most common types are the following:

synonyms	calm : peaceful :: anger : ire
opposites	praise : criticize :: hovel : mansion
degree	warm : hot :: grin : laugh
person : object	engineer : train :: pilot : airplane
function	car : garage :: airplane : hangar
order	dusk : night :: dawn : day
action : object	hoe : garden :: bake : cake
part : whole	leg : body :: stanza : poem

While it is not important that you verbalize the type of analogy you are working on, you may, if you get stuck on one, want to consider the type in order to determine the relationship between the words.

Roots, Prefixes, and Suffixes ///

To the person interested in words, a knowledge of roots, prefixes, and suffixes turns each new, unfamiliar word into a puzzle. And while it is a sure and life-long way to build your vocabulary, there are two points to keep in mind.

1. Some words evolved through usage so that today's definitions are different from what you might have inferred from an examination of their roots and/or prefixes. For example, the word abstruse contains the prefix "ab" (away) and the root "trudere" (to thrust) and literally means "to thrust away," but today the word is used to describe something that is "hard to understand."

2. Occasionally, you may go wrong on a root. For example, knowing that the root "vin" means to conquer, you would be correct in concluding that the word invincible means not able to be conquered; but if you tried to apply that root meaning to the word vindictive or vindicate, you would miss the mark. So, in analyzing an unfamiliar word, if your inferred meaning doesn't fit the context, check for other possible roots than the one you first assumed.

These warnings notwithstanding, a knowledge of roots and prefixes is the one best way to build a strong, vital vocabulary.

Reading Comprehension

Reading questions generally fall into several types.

1. *Identifying the main idea of the topic or the author's purpose.* In short, the question asks, "What is this selection about?"

In some paragraphs this is easy to spot because there are one or two ideas that leap from the paragraph. In some selections, however, this may be much more difficult where there are convoluted sentences with clauses embedded within clauses. It also may be difficult in those selections in which there are inverted sentences (a sentence with the subject at the end of the sentence) or elliptical sentences (a sentence in which a word is left out). All of these obstacles, however, can be overcome if the reader takes one sentence at a time and recasts it in his own words. Consider the following sentence:

> These writers either jot down their thoughts bit by bit, in short, ambiguous, and paradoxical sentences, which apparently mean much more than they say—of this kind of writing Schelling's treatises on natural philosophy are a splendid instance; or else they hold forth with a deluge of words and the most intolerable diffusiveness, as though no end of fuss were necessary to make the reader understand the deep meaning of their sentences, whereas it is some quite simple if not actually trivial idea, examples of which may be found in plenty in the popular works of Fichte, and the philosophical manuals of a hundred other miserable dunces.

But if we edit out some of the words, the main point of this sentence is obvious.

> These writers either jot down their thoughts bit by bit, in short sentences
>   which apparently mean much more than they say
>
>   or else they
> hold forth with a deluge of words   as though
>   [it]   were necessary to make the reader understand the deep meaning of their
> sentences, whereas it is   simple if not actually trivial idea.

While the previous sentence needed only deletions to make it clear, this next one requires major recasting and additions; that is, it must be read carefully and put into the reader's own words.

> Some in their discourse desire rather commendation of wit, in being able to hold all arguments, than of judgment, in discerning what is true; as if it were a praise to know what might be said, and not what should be thought.

After studying it, a reader might recast the sentence as follows:

> In their conversations, some people would rather win praise for their wit or style of saying something rather than win praise for their ability to judge between what is true or false—as if it were better to sound good regardless of the quality of thought.

2. *Identifying the stated or inferred meaning.* Simply, what is the author stating or suggesting?

3. *Identifying the tone or mood of the selection or the author's feeling.*

To answer this type of question, look closely at individual words and their connotations. For example, if an author describes one person as stubborn and another as firm, it tells you something of the author's feelings. In the same manner, if the author uses many words with harsh, negative connotations, he is conveying one mood; but if he uses words with milder negative connotations, he may be striving for quite another mood.

Lesson One

1. **appall** (ə pôl´) *verb*   to fill with horror or amazement; to shock
    The police were *appalled* at the huge number of homicides.
    syn: to horrify   *ant: to please, calm, or console*

2. **blasé** (blä zā´) *adj.*   uninterested; unexcited
    The millionaire seemed totally *blasé* at the idea of buying three new cars.
    syn: bored   *ant: awed*

3. **skeptical** (skĕp´ tĭ kəl) *adj.*   doubting or disbelieving
    Most people are *skeptical* of UFO's.
    syn: doubtful   *ant: convinced*

4. **nominal** (nŏm´ ə nəl) *adj.*   so small or low in relation to the real value as to be a mere token
    The bank transaction carried a *nominal* charge.
    syn: apparent, insignificant   *ant: actual, notable*

5. **persistent** (pər sĭs´ tĕnt) *adj.*   lasting; unceasing; persevering; enduring
    The boy was so *persistent* that his parents finally allowed him to go to the party.
    syn: stubborn; determined

6. **feint** (fānt) *verb*   to pretend in order to deceive an opponent, or divert attention away from
    the real target
    He scored the touchdown by *feinting* left and running right.
    syn: deceive, to make a deceptive movement; to trick

7. **whimsical** (wĭm´ sĭ kəl) *adj.*   playful; fanciful
    Cartoons are filled with *whimsical* characters.
                                              ant: serious

8. **integral** (ĭn´ tĭ grəl) *adj.*   necessary to form a whole
    Bow ties are *integral* parts of tuxedos.
    syn: important   *ant: unnecessary*

9. **lurid** (lŏŏr´ ĭd) *adj.*   causing shock or horror
    The victim gave a *lurid,* but accurate, account of the accident.
    syn: shocking; sensational   *ant: mild*

10. **seismic** (sīz´ mĭk) *adj.*   of, subject to, or caused by an earthquake or shock
    Ending the communist rule in Russia was an event of *seismic* proportions.
    syn: major   *ant: minor; unimportant*

Exercise I — Words in Context //

From the words below, supply the words needed to complete the sentences.

appall **blasé** **skeptical** **nominal** **persistent**

A. When it comes to investing my money, I am very cautious and _____ about new companies. My son, however, is the opposite and invests in a very _____ manner. Some corporations _____ me by their unethical behavior.

B. Although the telemarketer was _____, I refused the offer, even though she eliminated the _____ $15.00 sign-up fee.

From the words below, supply the words needed to complete the sentences.

feint **whimsical** **integral** **lurid** **seismic**

C. _____ to the peace treaty was a total surrender.

D. Most boxers could not _____ as well as Muhammad Ali.

E. The new comedy on TV had a funny, _____ character on it.

F. The earthquake produced _____ shocks felt thousands of miles away.

G. The _____, gruesome murder made national headlines.

Exercise II—Analogies //

Complete the analogy by choosing the most appropriate word.

1. male : female ::
    A. major : private
    B. dictionary : thesaurus
    C. steer : cow
    D. spring : summer

2. articulate : words ::
    A. freedom : democracy
    B. paint : colors
    C. prison : guards
    D. reveal : windows

3. capitol : legislation ::
    A. desk : participation
    B. pulpit : scorn
    C. school : education
    D. executive : presidential

Exercise III—Roots, Prefixes, and Suffixes //

What are the prefixes which are used in the following words?

incredible   unable   unarmed
disinterested   insincere   intolerant
uninvolved   disability   disadvantage

These prefixes, as you can easily see, are "in," "un," and "dis." They all mean "not." Therefore, when a word begins with any of these prefixes, the meaning is changed to a negative. List at least two more words for each prefix.

A.   in _____   un_____   dis_____
      in _____   un_____   dis _____
      in _____   un _____   dis _____

Sometimes, though, "in," "un," or "dis" are not prefixes, but are part of the word itself. "Intimate," "underneath," and "distinguish" are examples of this. Complete the spacs below with your own examples of words in which "in," "un," and "dis" are not used as prefixes, but are part of the words themselves.

B.   in _____   un _____   dis_____
      in _____   un _____   dis _____

Exercise IV—Reading Comprehension

Read the selection and answer the questions.

The guanaco, or wild llama, is found on the plains of Patagonia; it is the South American representative of the camel of the East. It is an elegant animal in a state of nature, with a long slender neck and fine legs. It is very common over the whole of the temperate parts of the continent, as far south as the islands near Cape Horn. It generally lives in small herds of from half a dozen to thirty in each; but on the banks of the St. Cruz we saw one herd which must have contained at least five hundred.

They are generally wild and extremely wary. Mr. Stokes told me that he one day saw through a glass a herd of these animals which evidently had been frightened, and were running away at full speed, although their distance was so great that he could not distinguish them with his naked eye. The sportsman frequently receives the first notice of their presence, by hearing from a long distance their peculiar shrill neighing note of alarm. If he then looks attentively, he will probably see the herd standing in a line on the side of some distant hill. On approaching nearer, a few more squeals are given, and off they set at an apparently slow, but really quick canter, along some narrow beaten track to a neighboring hill. If, however, by chance he abruptly meets a single animal, or several together, they will generally stand motionless and intently gaze at him; then perhaps move on a few yards, turn round, and look again.

By: Darwin
From: The Voyage of the Beagle

1. What is the best title for this selection?
   A. What Darwin Found
   B. Traits of Guanacos
   C. Mr. Stokes Spies a Llama
   D. Stalking the Wild Llamas
   E. Patagonian Wildlife

2. The difference between solitary and herding llamas is that single ones
   A. live in Patagonia.
   B. have longer necks.
   C. are extremely cautious.
   D. are less wary.
   E. can be shot more easily.

3. Darwin compares the llama to
   A. a quadruped.
   B. a mule.
   C. a camel.
   D. a guanaco.
   E. a herd of buffalo.

4. According to Darwin, the hunter
   A. can hear the llamas from a distance.
   B. has the advantage of a telescope.
   C. should not shoot these animals.
   D. can catch sight of llamas easily.
   E. needs to sneak up on llamas.

Lesson Two

1. **brazen** (brā´ zən) *adj.* rudely bold; impudent
   Elephants usually make a *brazen* but false charge at an enemy.
   syn: insolent   *ant: reserved, well-mannered*

2. **foster** (fô´ stər) *verb* to promote the development or growth of; to encourage, to cultivate
   Schools *foster* good citizenship as well as education.
   syn: to promote; to further; to aid   *ant: to oppose or restrain*

3. **impugn** (ĭm pyōōn´) *verb* to attack as false; to cast doubt on
   It was not necessary to *impugn* the accused's character in court.
   syn: deny   *ant: authenticate*

4. **obsolescence** (ŏb sə lĕs´ ənse) *noun* state of being no longer useful or in fashion
   Because nearly everyone uses computers, the typewriter may become an example of *obsolescence.*
   syn: outdatedness

5. **pretext** (prē´ tĕkst´) *noun* an excuse given to hide the real reason for something
   The officer's *pretext* for searching the car was that he had heard strange sounds coming from the trunk.
   syn: excuse; alibi

6. **singular** (sĭng´ gyə lər) *adj.* exceptional
   Superman, not Batman, is the *singular*, most-powerful superhero.
   syn: uncommon; unique   *ant: usual*

7. **sobriety** (sə brī´ ĭ tē) *noun* seriousness in bearing, manner, or treatment; absence of alcoholic intoxication
   The alcoholic longed for *sobriety*, but it eluded him.
        ant: intoxication

8. **ultimate** (ŭl´ tə mĭt) *adj.* final, conclusive; highest possible
   The *ultimate* goal of many amateur athletes is Olympic competition.
   syn: last; final   *ant: first, beginning*

9. **wan** (wŏn´) *adj.* unnaturally pale, as from illness; weak or faint
   Many people appear *wan* and tired after a harsh, cold, sunless winter.
   syn: ashen   *ant: colorful*

10. **wane** (wān´) *verb* to gradually decrease
    Directly after the moon is full, it begins to *wane*.
    syn: to abate; ebb   *ant: to wax; to grow*

Exercise I — Words in Context

From the words below, supply the words needed to complete the sentences.

impugn   **sobriety**   **ultimate**   **pretext**   **brazen**

A. In a(n) _____attempt to _____ the candidate's reputation, his opponent raised questions about the entire family's _____, not just the candidate's.

B. The invention of atomic power was voted the _____ event of the 20th century.

C. The dictator used false claims of invasion as a _____ for war.

From the words below, supply the words needed to complete the sentences.

obsolescence   **wane**   **wan**   **foster**   **singular**

D. The _____ difference between the twins is their height. After graduation, the competition between the two began to _____ gradually, and their new-found ease with each other was finally able to _____ peace within the family.

E. "You look rather _____ , even after a week in the sun," claimed my neighbor.

F. Complicated machinery frequently breaks down because of _____, not complexity.

Exercise II—Analogies

Complete the analogy by choosing the most appropriate word.

1. bovine : equine ::
   A. finger : digit
   B. steer : bull
   C. butterfly : insect
   D. cow : horse

2. acclaim : praise ::
   A. cowardice : fear
   B. love: hate
   C. capitulate : congratulate
   D. evoke : exhort

3. lawyer : client ::
   A. politician : candidate
   B. advisor : investor
   C. doctor : nurse
   D. plumber : leak

10

Exercise III—Roots, Prefixes, and Suffixes ///

What is the common root for the following words?

      technology   technique   technicality

This root "tech" means "skill," "art," or "craft." Therefore, when a word contains tis root, it has to do with some sort of ability.

List any words you can think of which contain "tech."

A.   _____   _____   _____

    _____   _____   _____

What is the common root for these words?

    revert   convert   vertigo   subvert   vertex

The root is "vert," and it means "turn." In the dictionary, look up the five words above to see how each word is derived from Latin and how each has the meaning of "turn."

Exercise IV—Reading Comprehension ///

Read the selection and answer the questions.

There is a spider crawling along the floor in the room where I sit; he runs with heedless, hurried haste, he hobbles awkwardly towards me, he stops—he sees the giant shadow before him, and, at a loss whether to retreat or proceed, meditates his huge foe—but since I do not stand up and seize him, as he would seize a hapless fly within his web, he takes heart, and ventures on with mingled cunning, impudence, and fear. As he passes me, I lift up the rug to assist his escape, for I am glad to get rid of the unwelcome intruder, and shudder at the recollection after he is gone. A child, a woman, a clown, or a moralist a century ago, would have crushed the little reptile to death—my philosophy has got beyond that—I bear the creature no ill-will, but still I hate the very sight of it. The spirit of malevolence survives the practical exertion of it. We learn to curb our will and keep our overt actions within the bounds of humanity, long before we can subdue our sentiments and imaginations to the same mild tone. We give up the external demonstration, the brute violence, but cannot part with the essence or principle of hostility.

From: On the Pleasure of Hating
By: William Hazlitt

1. What is the main idea of this selection?
   A. People generally hate spiders.
   B. It is wrong to hate.
   C. Hatred of evil is acceptable.
   D. Spiders are examples of peoples' hatred.
   E. People show hatred through emotions, not actions.

2. Which word is used *incorrectly* to describe the spider?
   A. fly
   B. reptile
   C. creature
   D. giant
   E. huge

3. Why does the author not kill the spider?
   A. He is not a cruel person.
   B. He does not act on impulse.
   C. He does not hate spiders.
   D. His philosophy has matured.
   E. He would rather allow it to live.

4. This passage examines differences between
   A. spiders and men.
   B. evil and hatred.
   C. hatred and reason.
   D. past and present.
   E. action and thought.

Lesson Three

1. **vapid** (văp´ĭd) *adj.* uninteresting ; flat; stale
    The wiretap revealed nothing but meaningless, *vapid* conversations.
    syn: flavorless; insipid   *ant: meaningful; zesty*

2. **unkempt** (ŭn kĕmpt´) *adj.* not neat or tidy
    During his absence, his lawn took on an *unkempt* appearance.
    syn: sloppy   *ant: neat*

3. **profane** (prə fān´) *adj.* showing contempt for God or sacred things
    For years the churches claimed any music not praising holiness was *profane*.
    syn: impious; irreverent   *ant: holy; sacred*

4. **premise** (prĕm´ĭs) *noun* a statement upon which an argument is based or from which a
    conclusion is drawn
    One of the first *premises* of American society is that all people are equal.
    syn: assumption

5. **potential** (pə tĕn´shəl) *noun* an ability that may or may not be developed
    Because of a poor attitude, the student never fulfilled his *potential*.
    syn: possibility   *ant: actuality*

6. **astute** (ə stōōt´) *adj.* keen in judgement
    An *astute* tenant does not sign a contract before reading it.
    syn: shrewd   *ant: gullible*

7. **jurisdiction** (jŏŏr´ĭs dĭk´shən) *noun* the authority to interpret and apply the law; the
    range of such authority
    The state police's *jurisdiction* ends at the border.
    syn: power

8. **innate** (ĭn´āt) *adj.* possessed from birth; inborn; inherent
    Some religions teach that everyone has an *innate* goodness.
    syn: natural   *ant: acquired*

9. **imperturbable** (ĭm´pər tûr´bə bəl) *adj.* not easily disturbed; unshakable; calm and
    collected
    A paramedic needs to be *imperturbable* or find a new job.
    syn: cool; composed   *ant: touchy; testy*

10. **duress** (dŏŏ rĕs´) *noun* constraint by threat; coercion
    The spy did not confess, even under *duress*.
    syn: force

Exercise I — Words in Context ///

From the words below, supply the words needed to complete the sentences.

innate   **vapid**   **astute**   **imperturbable**   **premise**

A.   The bigot's basic _____ is that one race is superior to another. This _____ assumption has no basis in fact. A more _____ reasoning would be that all races are equal, and that individuals vary in their _____ qualities.

B.   The stuntman looked _____ in the face of extreme danger.

From the words below, supply the words needed to complete the sentences.

duress   **jurisdiction**   **potential**   **profane**   **unkempt**

C.   The _____ vagrant was arrested, but he claimed the police had no _____ over him.

D.   The young child's _____ words surprised his parents.

E.   The prisoner-of-war claimed the confession he signed was made under _____ and torture.

F.   The drought greatly increased the _____ for forest fires.

Exercise II—Analogies ///

Complete the analogy by choosing the most appropriate word.

1. drink : thirst ::
    A. flay : fear
    B. harass : worry
    C. fret : anger
    D. consume : hunger

2. counselor : advice ::
    A. teacher : books
    B. coach : strategy
    C. host : party
    D. senator : debate

3. cake : mix ::
    A. whiskey : drink
    B. gasoline : refinery
    C. paper : read
    D. clothing : wash

Exercise III—Roots, Prefixes, and Suffixes ///

What is the suffix that the following words have in common?

debatable   reliable   callable   conceivable   miserable

This suffix means exactly what it says: "able to..." A variation of "able" is "ible," which means the same, as in "visible" or "horrible."

In nearly all cases, these two suffixes mean "capable of" or "able to." Can you find at least 10 other words which use these suffixes?

A.   _____able   _____ible
       _____able   _____ible
       _____able   _____ible
       _____able   _____ible
       _____able   _____ible

Exercise IV—Reading Comprehension

Read the selection and answer the questions.

A recent study reported that every five days an American child chokes to death on food, and the food most often choked on is the hot dog.

"If you were trying to design something that would be perfect to block a child's airway, it would be a bite-size piece of hot dog," says Dr. Susan P. Baker of Johns Hopkins University in Baltimore. Because they are round and soft, pieces of hot dog can easily plug the airway that opens into the esophagus. All a child has to do is cough, choke, or laugh while he is eating.

"A child under the age of four should not be given a whole hot dog to eat," Dr. Baker said. "Neither should they be cut crosswise. Most parents don't know that."

More than 40 percent of food choking deaths among children are caused by hot dogs, candy, nuts, or grapes, Dr. Baker reported in Friday's issue of the Journal of the American Medical Association. Half the choking deaths in infants younger than 12 months were caused by hot dogs, apple pieces, cookies, or biscuits.

Among one-year-olds–who suffered the highest incidents of food asphyxiation of all groups– carrots and hot dogs were most often the cause, the study found. Grapes and peanuts were the most frequent causes of fatal choking among two-year-olds. Among three-year-olds, only ten food fatalities occurred, but seven of them were blamed on hot dogs, the doctors said.

Dr. Baker recommended the following safety measures: change the shape of products to make them less dangerous; provide warning labels on packages; and put out information on high-risk foods to reduce the number of childhood choking cases.

A spokeswoman for Oscar Mayer Food said her company has looked into choking risks associated with hot dogs but has not modified its product or labels. "We feel that the major cause of the problem is lack of parental supervision when the children are eating," she said.

1. The best title for this article is
   A.   Dangerous Foods.
   B.   Don't Give Hot Dogs to Kids.
   C.   Hot Dogs Can Kill.
   D.   Cut Up Those Dogs.
   E.   Parents Should Observe Children's Food.

2. Which group had the most food deaths?
   A.   three-year-olds
   B.   two-year-olds
   C.   one-year-olds
   D.   The article does not say.

3. What can you infer from paragraph three?
   A.   Dr. Baker is a pediatric doctor.
   B.   Dr. Baker wants to prevent accidents.
   C.   Dr. Baker feels children under four should not eat hot dogs at all.
   D.   All the above
   E.   A and C are correct.

4. The hot dog spokesperson is
   A.   not concerned over the deaths.
   B.   a woman.
   C.   putting warning labels on the food.
   D.   going to change the shape of the food.
   E.   none of the above.

Lesson Four

1. **mundane** (mŭn dān´) *adj.* worldly; not spiritual
   Everyday *mundane* routines bored him.
   syn: commonplace   *ant: extraordinary*

2. **paltry** (pôl´ trē) *adj.* meager; insignificant
   We bought the food wholesale, for a *paltry* amount of money.
   syn: small; measly   *ant: significant*

3. **fray** (frā) *noun* fight
   Eager to join the *fray*, the crook punched someone.
   syn: brawl; scuffle

4. **scurry** (skûr´ē) *verb* to dash
   The bugs *scurried* when the light came on.
   syn: to scuttle; to dart

5. **feudal** (fyōōd´l) *adj.* pertaining to the Middle Ages
   No matter how rich the owner was, *feudal* castles were always cold.

6. **drudgery** (drŭj´ ə rē) *noun* difficult work
   He quit his boring job because of the *drudgery*.
   syn: labor; tediousness

7. **jostle** (jŏs´əl) *verb* to bump
   The last bowling pin had not been *jostled* enough to fall.
   syn: to push; to shove

8. **disperse** (dĭ-spûrs´) *verb* to scatter
   One drop of crude oil can be *dispersed* over gallons of fresh water.
   syn: to dispense; to spread   *ant: to gather*

9. **saturate** (sach´ ə-rāt´) *verb* to soak; to infuse
   Because the farmers had *saturated* the food with pesticides, we dared not eat it.
   syn: to drench   *ant: to dry out*

10. **vogue** (vōg) *noun* fashion
    The fashions in *vogue* today may be very out-of-step next season.
    syn: style; trend

Exercise I — Words in Context

From the words below, supply the words needed to complete the sentences.

| **scurry** | **paltry** | **drudgery** | **feudal** | **saturate** |

A. The servant's _____ each day was paid for with a _____ sum of money. She would _____ around the castle all day long, tired of the _____ system, which made her a serf.

B. Before cooking this meal, you must _____ the pan with oil.

From the words below, supply the words needed to complete the sentences.

| **disperse** | **vogue** | **jostled** | **fray** | **mundane** |

C. Years ago, proms in middle school were rare, but now they are very much in _____.

D. Ignore the _____ issues and concentrate on the important ones.

E. After a mild _____ had broken out during the football game, the police used tear gas to _____ the crowd; in the confusion people _____ one another in an effort to move away.

Exercise II—Analogies

Complete the analogy by choosing the most appropriate word.

1. county : state ::
   A. adolescence : adulthood
   B. clothing : attire
   C. infant : baby
   D. house : neighborhood

2. definition : dictionary ::
   A. magistrate : laws
   B. highway : map
   C. television : communication
   D. genius : intelligence

3. chorus : song ::
   A. stanza : poem
   B. meter : rhyme
   C. verse : line
   D. lyric : rhythm

Exercise III—Roots, Prefixes, and Suffixes

What is the root which is used in the following three words?

    contraband   contradictory   contrary

The root "contra" means "against." Usually, therefore, when a word has "contra" in it, it refers to being opposed to or in opposition to.

List three other words using "contra" as their root.

    A.   _____
           _____
           _____

Now, list a few words which have "contra" in them which do not mean "against," like *contraction*.

    B.   _____
           _____
           _____

Exercise IV—Reading Comprehension

Read the selection and answer the questions.

I know that in writing the following pages I am divulging the great secret of my life, the secret which for some years I have guarded far more carefully than any of my earthly possessions; and it is a curious study to me to analyze the motives which prompt me to do it. I feel that I am led by the same impulse which forces the unfound-out criminal to take somebody into his confidence, although he knows that the act is liable, even almost certain, to lead to his undoing. I know that I am playing with fire, and I feel the thrill which accompanies that most fascinating pastime; and, back of it all, I think I find a sort of savage and diabolical desire to gather up all the little tragedies of my life, and turn them into a practical joke on society.

And, too, I suffer a vague feeling of unsatisfaction, of regret, of almost remorse from which I am seeking relief, and of which I shall speak in the last paragraph of this account.

I was born in a little town of Georgia a few years after the close of the Civil War. I shall not mention the name of the town, because there are people still living there who could be connected with this narrative. I have only a faint recollection of the place of my birth. At times I can close my eyes, and call up in a dream-like way things that seem to have happened ages ago in some other world. I can see in this half vision a little house,— I am quite sure it was not a large one;— I can remember that flowers grew in the front yard, and that around each bed of flowers was a hedge of vary-colored glass bottles stuck in the ground neck down. I remember that once, while playing around in the sand, I became curious to know whether or not the bottles grew as the flowers did, and I proceeded to dig them up to find out; the investigation brought me a terrific spanking which indelibly fixed the incident in my mind.

From: Autobiography of an Ex-Colored Man
By: James Johnson

19

1. The "I" in this selection reveals emotions of
   A. worry and joy.
   B. sadness and anticipation.
   C. curiosity and unhappiness.
   D. relief and hatred.
   E. calmness and anger.

2. The name of the town where he was born is not discussed because
   A. his parents still live there.
   B. every reader would recognize it.
   C. it is in Georgia.
   D. he cannot recall it.
   E. people in the story are still in the town.

3. The author received a punishment for
   A. revealing names.
   B. throwing bottles.
   C. practical joking.
   D. ruining a flower bed.
   E. B and D are correct.

4. The best title for the FIRST PARAGRAPH ONLY would be
   A. Why I Write
   B. A Secret to Come
   C. Sharing the Unknown
   D. Earthly Possessions
   E. Thrills and Tragedies

1. **obstinate** (ŏb´ stə nĭt) *adj.* stubborn
    He argued with his mother about staying out late, but she was *obstinate* and set a curfew.
    syn: bull-headed   *ant: pliable*

2. **sally** (sal´ē) *noun* excursion
    Little Red Riding Hood went on a short *sally* to her grandmother's.
    syn: outing

3. **tranquil** (trang´kwəl) *adj.* calm
    The Pacific Ocean is not *tranquil* at all, yet its name does mean calm.
    syn: placid   *ant: agitated*

4. **pantheon** (pan´ thē-ŏn) *noun* a group of highly regarded people; a place for such people; a range
    The *pantheon* of religions goes from Animism to Zoroastrianism.

5. **placard** (plak´ ärd) *noun* sign
    Many men on strike held handwritten *placards*.
    syn: poster

6. **contrive** (kən-trīv´) *verb* to plot
    The swindler *contrived* ways to cheat the government.
    syn: to concoct; to devise

7. **constraint** (kən stränt´) *noun* force; coercion
    I realize that you may be upset, Bob, but show some *constraint* and behave yourself.
    syn: restraint

8. **equilibrium** (ē kwəlĭb´ rē-əm) *noun* balance; stability
    Mark Twain achieved the perfect *equilibrium* between humor and satire.
    syn: steadiness; evenness   *ant: out of balance*

9. **exponential** (ĕkspo nĕn´ shəl) *adj.* increasing rapidly
    The universe has expanded in an *exponential* fashion since it began.

10. **dupe** (do͞op) *verb* to fool; to delude
    Many sweepstakes use trickery to *dupe* people into entering.
    syn: to hoax; to trick

Exercise I — Words in Context

From the words below, supply the words needed to complete the sentences.

dupe	contrived	obstinate	equilibrium	pantheon

A.   "We tried to _____ him out of his money," said the swindlers, "but he was so _____ that we gave up."

B.   At the head of the _____ of Greek gods sat Zeus.

C.   An ear infection can cause a loss of _____.

D.   The children _____ a swing simply from three hanging vines.

From the words below, supply the words needed to complete the sentences.

placard	sally	exponential	constraints	tranquil

E.   The night was so _____ and warm even my mother was able to _____ forth into it.

F.   The _____ had profanity on it.

G.   Inflation can cause prices to rise in a(n) _____ manner.

H.   Many _____ were heaped upon the boy for violating curfew.

Exercise II—Analogies

Complete the analogy by choosing the most appropriate word.

1. lawyer : argument ::
   A. tyrant : army
   B. humorist : fight
   C. servant : clean
   D. carpenter : hammer

2. inconsequential : significant ::
   A. lazy : energetic
   B. relevant : important
   C. feud : treaty
   D. leader : worshipper

3. flippant : disrespectful ::
   A. real : actual
   B. allude : gainsay
   C. column : pillory
   D. pretend : disbelieve

Exercise III—Roots, Prefixes, and Suffixes ///

What prefix is common to the following words?

transatlantic   translation   transfer   transmit

You can easily see that the root is "trans." It means "across." List at least 5 more words using this prefix.

A.   _____   _____
      _____   _____
      _____   _____

A set of useful prefixes is "hypo" and "hyper." These are easily confused; one (**hypo**) means "under" and the other (**hyper**) means "over" or "above." A needle under your skin is a _____dermic. Another word for high blood pressure, above normal, is _____tension. List some words you already know which use these prefixes.

B.   hyper _____   hypo_____
      hyper _____   hypo_____
      hyper _____   hypo_____

Exercise IV—Reading Comprehension ///

Read the selection and answer the questions.

For years, farmers have known that pigs love to play with toys. They also know that pigs that are given toys to play with are healthier, calmer, and easier to handle. Now research has set out to discover exactly which type of toys pigs prefer.

"There is no point in wasting money on toys for pigs if the pigs are not going to play with them," said Peter Knight, a biologist who studies animal behavior. He has been studying pigs for the past seven years. Through his research he hopes to find ways to boost America's production of high-quality pork.

"People think of pigs as being fat, stupid, dirty animals, who spend most of their time lying in the mud eating," said Knight. "The fact is pigs are one of the smartest of all animals. They are certainly much smarter than dogs. But if they are just kept penned up all the time with nothing to do, they get bored and frustrated. In this, they are just like people."

Knight explained that pigs that are bored tend to get into fights. They bite each other's tails and otherwise hurt each other. In addition, they are harder to get ready for market and more difficult to unload for the slaughterhouse.

More importantly, however, "pigs that get excited and violent tend to produce poor quality meat." Giving them toys keeps their minds occupied. "This way they stay calmer and don't get into fights," said Knight.

But what kind of toys do pigs prefer? According to Knight's research, two of the toys which are favorites among farmers are not favorites with the pigs. "Farmers often give pigs bowling balls," said Knight. "At first, the pigs enjoy butting against them with their heads, and rolling the balls around their pens. But eventually, the balls become coated with manure. Then the pigs ignore them."

Another old favorite of farmers who raise pigs is the dangling chain. This is left hanging over the pig's pen. "We found that chains were too heavy and hurt the pigs' mouths. They much prefer strips of cloth or rubber hoses hanging above their pens," said Knight.

According to Knight, some pigs chew on the ends of the cloth or hoses like chewing gum. Others jerk and shake them the way a puppy shakes a rag doll. "When the pigs have toys they like, they play with them regularly," said Knight. "When we first introduced them to toys, they played with them for about an hour a day. After a week or so, they gradually tapered off to about a half an hour a day of intense activity."

Knight's findings are already being put into practice by some hog raisers. "It is a heck of a lot cheaper to give the pigs a few old rubber hoses than it is to buy them bowling balls," said Gene Green of Wisconsin. Green has raised hogs for 15 years.

"And if it keeps the pigs happy, then I'll have less trouble with them and they will get into fewer fights. I'm putting in some rubber hoses for them today."

The second phase of Knight's research starts soon. Now he is trying to determine if the kind of toys the pigs plays with affects the quality and quantity of meat the pig produces. "We know that giving the pigs toys doesn't *hurt* weight gain, but we don't know yet whether it will *help* weight gain," he said.

1. What fact is not in the article?
   A. Pigs like toys.
   B. Pigs are smarter than dogs.
   C. Pigs gain weight through playing with toys.
   D. Mr. Knight first used bowling balls as pig toys.
   E. Pigs never fight.

2. How are hanging chains different from hanging cloth?
   A. Pigs prefer the metal.
   B. Chains interfere with the bowling balls.
   C. Cloth can fall into the pens.
   D. Chains hurt pigs' mouths.
   E. Chains are harder to hang.

3. Gene Green has
   A. determined that pork tastes better if pigs are content.
   B. raised pigs for 15 years.
   C. seen pigs bite each other's tails.
   D. experimented first with chains.
   E. disagrees with Knight's findings.

4. What can you infer from the article?
   A. Pigs are easily bored.
   B. Hogs prefer hoses to chains.
   C. Happy hogs make for better meat.
   D. All the above are correct
   E. A, and B are correct

Lesson Six

1. **spontaneous** (spŏn tā´ nē-əs) *adj.* happening without an external cause
   When the magician and his assistant disappeared, the audience gave them a *spontaneous* ovation.
   syn: self-generated; unplanned   *ant: premeditated*

2. **cope** (kōp) *verb* to deal with
   It's easier to *cope* with success than failure.
   syn: to contend with

3. **wither** (wĭth´ ər) *verb* to dry up; to shrivel
   The young plants *withered* without water.
   syn: to lose moisture; to shrink   *ant: to moisten; to wet*

4. **valor** (val´ ər) *noun* bravery
   The soldiers were rewarded for their *valor* in the battle.
   syn: courage   *ant: cowardice*

5. **assail** (ə-sāl´) *verb* to attack
   While the Army *assailed* the enemy from the inland side, the Navy hit the coast.
   syn: to assault   *ant: to retreat*

6. **taut** (tôt´) *adj.* tight; tense
   The play's dialogue was so *taut*, the audience was on the edge of their seats.
   syn: rigid   *ant: loose; slack*

7. **stunt** (stŭnt) *verb* to limit growth
   People used to believe cigarettes would *stunt* children's growth.
   syn: to dwarf; to check

8. **assets** (as´ĕts) *noun* resources or wealth
   All his financial and business *assets* belonged to his wife.
   syn: credits; money   *ant: liabilities; handicaps*

9. **potent** (pōt´nt) *adj.* powerful
   Alcohol and some medicines produce a *potent* reaction, which can kill.
   syn: strong   *ant: weak*

10. **saga** (sä´ gə) *noun* story; tale
    One of the best-known movie *sagas* is the *Star Trek* series.
    syn: epic

Exercise I — Words in Context

From the words below, supply the words needed to complete the sentences.

wither	valor	taut	stunt	assail

A. They were able to successfully _____ the fortress only because of the great _____ of many soldiers.

B. A lack of proper nourishment may _____ a child's growth.

C. During droughts, many fruits _____ on the vines.

D. "Pull that line _____," yelled the boss.

From the words below, supply the words needed to complete the sentences.

assets	cope	potent	saga	spontaneous

E. Beware of the snake's _____ venom.

F. Because the government's seizure of all their_____plunged then into poverty, the couple could not _____ with life.

G. _____ applause broke out during the song.

H. The _____ of Ulysses' twenty-year journey was written by Homer.

Exercise II—Analogies

Complete the analogy by choosing the most appropriate word.

1. voice : sing ::
   A. apple : eat
   B. jog : walk
   C. feet : dance
   D. worm : ground

2. extinct : flourish ::
   A. triangular : parallel
   B. regular : everyday
   C. anniversary : wedding
   D. holy : desecrate

3. commercial : nonprofit ::
   A. change : similarity
   B. descent : repel
   C. homicide : patricide
   D. collapse : remove

Exercise III—Roots, Prefixes, and Suffixes

    communism   consumerism
    materialism   impressionism
    baptism   capitalism

The suffix on all these words, "ism," means a "theory, action, or characteristic." Many words have this suffix attached to them. List five words you know which have "ism" on the end.

A. _____ism   _____ism

    _____ism   _____ism

    _____ism

Another suffix, "ary," is related to "ism." It means "related to" or "connected to."

complimentary - related to a compliment
boundary   - connected to the bounds of something
aviary   - related to avians (birds)
parliamentary - connected with a parliament
dictionary   - related to speech

List five words which end in this way.

B. _____ary   _____ary

    _____ary   _____ary

    _____ary

Exercise IV—Reading Comprehension

Read the selection and answer the questions.

For a quarter, visitors to Clyde Peeling's Reptileland can watch a little open door open, a live cricket fall into a terrarium and a frog gobble up the insect. "But the machine was not made to thrill sick people," Peeling said. "Rather, it was made to educate people about a fact of life. In nature there are hunters and the hunted, the predators and the prey."

"No one has made a machine that dispenses live animals to predators before," said Peeling, 41, who has owned the two-acre reptile zoo for 20 years. "I see it as an educational tool. It is not only good because the amphibians and reptiles get to eat live insects, but you have to make people face the facts. If you eat a hamburger, someone has to kill a cow," he said.

While some people find the idea repulsive, some zoo curators see it as a possible answer to two of their big problems. John Behler of the City Zoo said, "The two biggest problems facing zoos are educating the public and feeding the animals. This machine does both; it has some exciting possibilities," he said.

Behler, who plans to buy three cricket machines for the City Zoo, said even sadists drawn to the machines will walk away with a valuable lesson. "Whoever is doing this activity will learn the value of insectivores and the large number of insects, often harmful, they eat. Whether from fun or entertainment, they will learn a valuable lesson."

Peeling said he began talking with his father about developing the machine several years ago. He got the idea after getting fed up with zoo visitors complaining about listless reptiles. "Some animals, if there is nothing to eat, there is nothing to do. It occurred to me that if we could feed them in some way acceptable to the public, it would go over big."

1. Why was the machine developed?
   A. to make money
   B. to make animals seem less lazy
   C. to feed some animals
   D. A, B, and C
   E. B and C

2. Which pair of words describe the same thing?
   A. "insectivore," "curator"
   B. "predator," "prey"
   C. "curator," "listless"
   D. "repulsive," "reptile"
   E. "hunters," "predators"

3. Peeling
   A. bought the idea of the machine from his father.
   B. owns a reptile zoo.
   C. wants to thrill people.
   D. earns a lot of money from his machine.
   E. All the above are correct.

4. What point is made about cows?
   A. Cows do not eat insects.
   B. Cows should be in some zoos.
   C. Cows are slaughtered for meat.
   D. Cows are no different from crickets.
   E. People should not eat meat.

Lesson Seven

1. **undermine** (ŭn dər mīn´) *verb* to weaken; to ruin
   During war, each side attempts to *undermine* and eventually destroy its enemy's will to fight.
   syn: to wreck; to thwart   *ant: to reinforce*

2. **terminal** (tûr´ mə-nəl) *adj.* last
   He paid the full fare and rode the bus until the *terminal* stop .
   syn: final   *ant: first; beginning*

3. **spew** (spyōō) *verb* to spit out
   The bank robber *spewed* curses at the police.
   syn: to gush

4. **scrutinize** (skrōōt´ n īz) *verb* to examine
   IRS agents needed to *scrutinize* the company's records.
   syn: to study

5. **savory** (sā´ və-rē) *adj.* tempting; tasty
   The restaurant's desserts were so *savory* that we had seconds.
   syn: sweet; fragrant   *ant: unpalatable*

6. **rejuvenate** (rǐ jōō´ və-nāt) *verb* to make youthful again
   The trip to Hawaii *rejuvenated* the overworked housewife.
   syn: to renew   *ant: to age*

7. **realm** (rĕlm) *noun* range; scope
   His outrageous lie was so far beyond the *realm* of reality that we laughed aloud.
   syn: world

8. **badger** (baj´ ər) *verb* to bother
   Even though it was weaned, the young colt still *badgered* his mother for milk.
   syn: to hound; to plague   *ant: to leave alone*

9. **belittle** (bǐ-lǐt´l) *verb* to criticize; to diminish
   Our sarcastic teacher constantly *belittled* the students.
   syn: to disparage; to detract   *ant: to magnify; to praise*

10. **concoct** (kən-kŏkt´) *verb* to contrive; to devise
    The writers *concocted* a new dilemma for the hero to overcome each week.
    syn: to invent; to conceive

Exercise I — Words in Context

From the words below, supply the words needed to complete the sentences.

concoct	**badger**	**spewed**	**terminal**	**savory**

A.   The kitchen emitted many _____ smells; each day the chefs tried to _____ new recipes.

B.   A period is the _____ punctuation mark of declarative sentences.

C.   "Don't _____ me with dumb questions," screamed the impatient mother.

D.   The erupting volcano _____ tons of lava on the village.

From the words below, supply the words needed to complete the sentences.

realm	**undermined**	**rejuvenated**	**belittle**	**scrutinize**

E.   Marine biologists _____ the underwater _____ to find new species.

F.   The chemical spill near the laboratory _____ years of work.

G.   His new artificial knee _____ the elderly man's spirits.

H.   If you constantly _____ friends, expect to lose them.

Exercise II—Analogies

Complete the analogy by choosing the most appropriate word.

1. communication : word ::
    A. feast : famine
    B. belief : thought
    C. season : bloom
    D. ridiculous : practical

2. thin : obese ::
    A. awake : conscious
    B. harmony : discord
    C. emotional : sad
    D. avid : eager

3. bother : harass ::
    A. contrast : oppose
    B. increase : rely
    C. angle : acute
    D. blatant : concealed

Exercise III—Roots, Prefixes, and Suffixes

Look at the prefixes for these words and figure out what each word means.

A.
1. prejudice   to_____
2. prefix   a _____
3. premedical   _____
4. predetermine   to_____
5. precook   to_____

The prefix "pre" means "before," "ahead," or "in front of." In almost all uses of "pre," it changes the meaning of the root of the word. Some words, though, have "pre" not used as a prefix, but as an essential part of the word. "Pregnant" is a word like this. It does not mean "before" at all. Separate the following list into two columns, one in which "pre" means "prior to" as a prefix, and one in which "pre" is part of the word itself.

B.
precious   preach   prehistoric
predator   precise   precaution
premeditated   prebuilt   preamplifier
premier

"pre" as prefix to words   "pre" as part of words

1. _____   6. _____
2. _____   7. _____
3. _____   8. _____
4. _____   9. _____
5. _____   10. _____

Exercise IV—Reading Comprehension

Read the selection and answer the questions.

Every year the United States sends billions of dollars overseas for foreign aid and military operations trying to bring peace and prosperity to troubled regions around the world. Your help often comes too late and seldom alleviates the root of the problem.

Overcrowding and rapid population growth exacerbates many causes of conflict around the world, like ethnic tensions, economic disparity, and struggle over scarce resources. The population of our planet has ballooned rapidly from 2 billion in 1935 to almost 6 billion today, and will reach 8 billion by 2025. Ninety percent of this growth will occur in the most troubled regions of the Third World, increasing their already difficult tasks of peace and economic development.

Speaker: Helmut Kohl

1. The main idea expressed here is
   A. the U.S. spends money wastefully.
   B. world population is a problem.
   C. a scarcity of natural resources exists.
   D. the Third World has numerous problems.
   E. foreign military aid is unnecessary.

2. The word "exacerbates" (paragraph 2, line 1) probably means
   A. increases
   B. decreases
   C. worsens
   D. lessens
   E. alleviates

3. World population in 1935 was approximately
   A. 2 billion
   B. 4 billion
   C. 6 billion
   D. 8 billion
   E. answer cannot be determined

4. Peace is hurt, according to this passage, by
   A. ethnic tensions.
   B. scarce resources.
   C. economic problems.
   D. expanding population.
   E. all the above are correct.

Lesson Eight

1. **condolence** (ken dō´ləns) *noun* sympathy
   The funeral director offered *condolences* to relatives of the deceased.
   syn: compassion   *ant: harshness*

2. **candor** (kan´ dər) *noun* honesty
   His *candor* and honesty impressed everyone who knew him.
   syn: truthfulness   *ant: deceit*

3. **buff** (bŭf) *noun* enthusiast
   The knowledgeable art *buff* somehow mistook a Rembrandt for a fake.
   syn: fan; aficionado

4. **composure** (kəm pō´ zhar) *noun* calmness
   In a fire, keep your *composure* and do not panic.
   syn: coolness   *ant: panic*

5. **prestigious** (prě stē´ jəs) *adj.* famous; notable
   I once received a *prestigious* award for my essay on politics.
   syn: distinguished   *ant: unknown*

6. **replenish** (rĭ-plĕn´ ĭsh) *verb* to restore
   Our dog loves biscuits, and we must *replenish* her supply weekly.
   syn: to replace   *ant: to use up*

7. **repress** (rĭ-prĕs´) *verb* to suppress; to control
   The majority frequently tries to *repress* the rights of the minority.
   syn: to restrain   *ant: to give free rein*

8. **ruse** (rōōs´) *noun* trick; ploy
   Children's games are filled with *ruses* and surprises.
   syn: maneuver; gimmick

9. **ruthless** (rōōth´lĭs) *adj.* merciless; grim
   We were put on a *ruthless* program of exercise and diet.
   syn: unrelenting

10. **procrastinate** (prō kras´tə-nāt) *verb* to delay
    The test was tomorrow, but Dallas *procrastinated* studying for it until the last minute.
    syn: to put off; to postpone

33

Exercise I — Words in Context ///

From the words below, supply the words needed to complete the sentences.

ruthless **repress** **ruse** **condolence** **candor**

A. One _____ gangster used a clever _____ to avoid capture; he had his gang members send letters of _____ to his wife to convince police he had been killed.

B. The psychiatrist told her patient not to _____ any emotions but to express them with complete _____.

From the words below, supply the words needed to complete the sentences.

procrastinate **buff** **composure** **replenish** **prestigious**

C. He was accepted to a _____ university.

D. If you _____ much longer, you'll miss your deadline.

E. After exercise, _____ your body's store of water.

F. The Civil War _____ discovered a relic of Gettysburg on his property and totally lost his _____ because of it.

Exercise II—Analogies ///

Complete the analogy by choosing the most appropriate word.

1. decade : eon ::
   A. book : page
   B. city : continent
   C. library : books
   D. seasoning : pepper

2. analogous : similar ::
   A. arable : farmable
   B. bigoted: spiteful
   C. destructive : constructive
   D. amenable : possible

3. doleful : sad ::
   A. walk : jog
   B. gasoline : car
   C. race : prejudice
   D. hilarious : happy

Exercise III—Roots, Prefixes, and Suffixes

What is the common root in the following words, and what do you think it means?

> territorial
> terrain
> terrace
> terrarium
> Mediterranean

The root "terr" means "earth" or "land." All the words above refer to that idea. The prefix in the last word "medi" means middle; as such, a few thousand years ago, the Mediterranean Sea must have been considered the _____ of the _____. List at least 5 words which use "terr" to mean "land" and a few which do not.

A.   _____   _____   _____
             _____   _____   _____
             _____   _____   _____

Exercise IV—Reading Comprehension

Read the selection and answer the questions.

Smokeless tobacco use also predicts other drug use. In a study of more than 3,000 male adolescents interviewed twice at nine-month intervals about their use of various psychoactive substances, the main findings were that (1) smokeless tobacco users were significantly more likely to use cigarettes, marijuana, or alcohol than nonusers, (2) users of smokeless tobacco were significantly more likely to take up the use of these other substances by the second interview if they were not using them at the first, and (3) adolescents who were using any of these substances at the first interview were significantly more likely to increase their use of the substance if they also used smokeless tobacco.

Two other facts are important to consider when evaluating the role of smokeless tobacco products in the use of cigarettes and other substances. First, the overall impact of smokeless tobacco is currently limited primarily to males (the main users of these substances). Second, smokeless tobacco users tend to initiate their tobacco use at about the same age as cigarette smokers or at a slightly earlier age.

1. The best title for this article is
    A. Smoking Leads To Drug Use.
    B. Tobacco Usage Increases.
    C. Smokeless Tobacco Use On The Rise.
    D. Smokeless Tobacco Use Predicts Other Drug Use.
    E. Three Thousand Adolescents Use Smokeless Tobacco.

2. One conclusion reached by the article is that
    A. males are the main users of smokeless tobacco.
    B. use of smokeless tobacco is unrelated to use of other drugs.
    C. users of smokeless tobacco start at a later age than cigarette smokers.
    D. two interviews are necessary.
    E. smokeless tobacco use begins in high school.

3. The word "psychoactive" (paragraph 1 line 2) refers to
    A. all drugs.
    B. drugs besides those in smokeless tobacco.
    C. alcohol.
    D. marijuana.
    E. cigarettes.

4. From this study we may infer that
    A. not many females use drugs.
    B. smoking is an easy habit to break.
    C. smokeless tobacco is less harmful than other forms of tobacco.
    D. users of smokeless tobacco are likely to use other substances.

Lesson Nine

1. **abortive** (ə bôr´tĭv) *adj.* premature; fruitless
   The airplane was forced to make an *abortive* landing in the blizzard.
   syn: rudimentary; unsuccessful   *ant: consummated*

2. **accost** (ə kôst´) *verb* to confront; to challenge
   The mugger *accosted* his victims only at night.
   syn: to approach boldly

3. **acute** (ə-kyōōt´) *adj.* serious; sharp
   Boris contracted an *acute* case of food poisoning, which landed him in the hospital.
   syn: critical; crucial   *ant: dull*

4. **debris** (də-brē´) *noun* wreckage; ruins
   The *debris* from the hurricane's destruction lay at her feet.
   syn: garbage; junk; rubble

5. **decade** (dĕk´ād) *noun* a period of ten years
   After a *decade* of obscurity, Richard Nixon again emerged as a political force.

6. **deploy** (dĭ-ploi´) *verb* to spread out; to arrange
   During the riot, extra police were *deployed* around the city.
   syn: to move strategically; scatter

7. **genre** (zhän´rə) *noun* kind; sort; style; class
   Of the many different *genres* of literature we studied, I liked poetry the best.
   syn: category

8. **guise** (gīz) *noun* external appearance
   On Halloween, many youngsters go out in the *guise* of witches.
   syn: aspect; style of dress; pretext

9. **gusto** (gŭs´tō) *noun* zest; relish
   Spot, the tiny dog, ate her treats with great *gusto*.
   syn: enjoyment; zeal   *ant: dislike*

10. **matron** (mā´trən) *noun* a woman in charge
    Contrary to my expectations, the *matron* at the prison was a small, slim woman.

11. **meager** (mē´gər) *adj.* small amount
    The storm ruined all but a *meager* amount of our food.
    syn: inadequate   *ant: sufficient*

12. **puny** (pyōō´nē) *adj.* less than normal size and strength
    Following years of weight-lifting, his *puny* body was transformed greatly.
    syn: weak; small

13. **quarry** (kwôr´ē) *noun*   the object of a search
Ponce de Leon's *quarry* was the fictitious "fountain of youth."
syn: hunted

14. **sordid** (sôr´dĭd) *adj.*   dirty; filthy
The police uncovered a *sordid* scheme to blackmail the senator.
syn: squalid; dishonorable   *ant: clean; honorable*

15. **spate** (spāt) *noun*   a sudden flood or outpouring: series
For a while, a *spate* of killings terrified the community.
syn: flow

Exercise I — Words in Context

From the words below, supply the words needed to complete the sentences.

puny	**abortive**	**debris**	**matron**	**genre**

A.   There was a great deal of _____ left after the storm.

B.   The folk singing _____ long ago gave way to hard rock.

C.   After a(n) _____ attempt to overthrow her harsh authority, the elderly _____ tightened her restrictive rules.

D.   Despite looking _____, Al easily lifted the heavy safe.

From the words below, supply the words needed to complete the sentences.

sordid	**accosted**	**decade**	**guise**	**meager**

E.   Sheila tried to keep the _____ details of her arrest quiet; they had followed her for years, and her _____ efforts accomplished little.

F.   Over the past _____, the outer islands have been _____ by many storms. Some were huge, but others sneaked in, without detection, in the _____ of a simple thunderstorm.

From the words below, supply the words needed to complete the sentences.

gusto	**quarry**	**spate**	**acute**	**deploy**

G.   The escaped prisoner eluded the police for hours, so they decided to _____ bloodhounds for assistance. The dogs searched for the man with _____ and with loud barking. Their _____, though, had the luck of a heavy _____ of rain. Even the dogs' well-known, _____ sense of smell could not help.

38

Exercise II—Analogies

Complete the analogy by choosing the most appropriate word.

1. tranquility : hostility ::
   A. peace : surrender
   B. condemnation : applause
   C. trite : obvious
   D. wall : roof

2. ski : snow ::
   A. race : distance
   B. fun : game
   C. pool : swim
   D. swim : water

3. virtuoso : practice ::
   A. dancer : music
   B. surgeon : study
   C. zealot : martyr
   D. saint : repudiation

Exercise III—Roots, Prefixes, and Suffixes

moronic	A. _____
acidic	B. _____
allergic	C. _____
meteoric	D. _____
cosmic	E. _____
dramatic	F. _____

As you can see, all the words above end in the suffix "ic," which means "relating to" or "characterized by." Define the words above in the spaces provided.

A word like "electronic" has as its literal definition "related to electrons." You may not know that we get electric power from moving electrons, but knowing the suffix helps you understand the word. Now below, write a list of at least six words ending with the suffix "ic."

G. _____   _____   _____

_____   _____   _____

Exercise IV—Reading Comprehension

Read the selection and answer the questions.

An early NASA study focused on the question, "How can a manned base be established on the moon?" The first step was to perform a Transportation Analysis and determine the most advantageous method of transporting men and materials to the moon and returning the men to earth. All conceivable chemical, nuclear and ion propulsion systems, using earth and lunar satellites, as well as "direct shot" trajectories, were considered. In addition, every reasonable technical perturbation was considered. *As a result of the analysis it was conclusively shown that the "direct shot" to the moon, using a five stage chemically propelled vehicle, is the most desirable.* This was not the expected conclusion since the establishment and use of a manned earth satellite-refueling station has been proposed for many years as the best way for man to travel to the moon. However, these original proposals did not have the benefit of a detailed analysis like the one performed in this study.

The analysis indicated the nuclear propulsion system could not be operational before 1970, so it was not advisable to rely on this system to establish the lunar base. However, if a nuclear system is available as expected, it could be used as indicated on the NASA Master Program Schedule to logistically support the base.

1. The best title for this selection is
    A. Establishment of Moon Proposals.
    B. Analysis of the Moon Proposals.
    C. To the Moon and Back.
    D. Moon Shot Study Points Out Possibilities.
    E. Nuclear Power to Supply Moon Base.

2. A direct shot at the moon was
    A. dropped in favor of a five-stage vehicle.
    B. an unexpected conclusion.
    C. attempted previously.
    D. abandoned because of its cost.
    E. propellable through nuclear power.

3. The word "perturbation" (line 5) probably means
    A. variability.
    B. worry.
    C. advancement.
    D. miracle.
    E. mission.

4. NASA implies that nuclear power could provide the energy if that kind of power
    A. were safe.
    B. were ready in time.
    C. would supply the needs of the space craft.
    D. worked best.
    E. the answer cannot be determined.

Lesson Ten

1. **yen** (yĕn) *noun*   desire
    My cat has a strange *yen* for eating corn on the cob.
    syn: longing

2. **somber** (sŏm´bər) *adj.*   dark; gloomy
    The *somber* weather report predicted a major storm approaching.
    syn: bleak   *ant: cheerful*

3. **prudent** (prōōd´nt) *adj.*   wise; careful
    The most *prudent* route across the mountains proved to be easier than the others.
    syn: sensible   *ant: careless*

4. **culprit** (kŭl´prĭt) *noun*   guilty person
    Ellen finally discovered the *culprit* who stole her lunch.
    syn: suspect

5. **gazebo** (gə-zē´bō) *noun*   small building
    Everyone admired the small, beautiful *gazebo* in our backyard.
    syn: summerhouse; pagoda

6. **solace** (sŏl´əs) *noun*   comfort; cheer
    A crying infant receives love and *solace* from its mother.
    syn: consolation

7. **siren** (sī´rən) *noun*   attractive woman
    The latest, young, movie *siren* to become a star could also act very well.

8. **mastiff** (măs´tĭf) *noun*   large dog
    Surprisingly, the prices for the giant *mastiff* and the miniature poodle were the same.

9. **mar** (mär) *verb*   to damage; to harm
    One suspension may *mar* your record and hurt your college acceptance chances.
    syn: to spoil; to scar   *ant: to beautify*

10. **gaudy** (gô´dē) *adj.*   vulgarly showy
    They filled the gym with many *gaudy* decorations for the spring dance.
    syn: brazen; flashy   *ant: restrained; tasteful*

11. **adverse** (ad-vûrs´) *adj.*   antagonistic; harmful or unfavorable
    The patient's *adverse* reaction to penicillin nearly killed him.
    syn: impeding   *ant: positive; satisfactory*

12. **detriment** (dĕt´rə-mənt) *noun*   disadvantage; harm
    Color blindness is usually a *detriment* in becoming a pilot.
    syn: drawback; handicap   *ant: advantage; benefit*

13. **harass** (hăr´ əs) *verb* to bother; to plague
    When the birds swoop down and *harass* the tiny cat, she runs up on the porch.
    syn: to badger; to hound

14. **facilitate** (fə sĭl´ ĭ tāt) *verb* to ease
    To *facilitate* painting our house, we moved all the furniture into one room.
    syn: to help   *ant: to obstruct*

15. **irk** (ûrk) *verb* to irritate; to bother
    We checked into the hotel, but the dirt left in our room *irked* us greatly.
    syn: to annoy

Exercise I — Words in Context

From the words below, supply the words needed to complete the sentences.

yen	somber	prudent	culprit	gazebo

A. The sky grew _____ with the appearance of dark clouds and snow. Winter often gave the whole family a(n) _____ to fly to a tropical island, where they could escape the horrid weather, sit inside a white_____, and soak up the atmosphere.

B. "It's never _____ to cheat on an exam," the teacher stated as she stared directly at the suspected _____ .

From the words below, supply the words needed to complete the sentences.

solace	siren	mastiff	marred	gaudy

C. The huge _____ strode down the avenue like she owned it; her collar, covered with _____ ribbons, however, betrayed her as a mere house pet, who wouldn't hurt a fly.

D. The preacher spoke quietly to the crying woman, offering _____ with words from the Bible.

E. My car's windows were totally _____ with soap last Halloween.

F. In ancient times people believed a tempting _____ could bewitch men.

From the words below, supply the words needed to complete the sentences.

adverse	detriment	harass	facilitate	irked

G. All the _____ publicity over the mayor's fine for littering gave the townspeople the opportunity to _____ him as spokesman for the "Beautify Our Town" committee. It acted as a(n) _____ to all he had previously accomplished, which _____ him greatly. His plan to _____ his political aspirations through environmental issues backfired on him.

Exercise II—Analogies

Complete the analogy by choosing the most appropriate word.

1. engine : motorcycle ::
   A. propeller : boat
   B. brick : wall
   C. snake : reptile
   D. sentence : paragraph

2. dove : peace ::
   A. genocide : Nazi
   B. cross : Christianity
   C. cigarette : cancer
   D. teacher : education

3. morose : depressed ::
   A. nebulous : clear
   B. major : minor
   C. listless : exhausted
   D. overjoyed : happy

Exercise IV—Reading Comprehension

Read the selection and answer the questions.

Are the penny's days numbered? Will we soon be saying, "a nickel saved is a nickel earned"? The question comes up because Congress is thinking about stopping production of the penny. Some Congressmen say the penny costs the government more money to make than the coin is worth.

A fact-finding federal panel says that getting rid of the one-cent piece would save taxpayers $70 million a year. Every year, more than five billion pennies–that's $50 million–disappear from circulation. Most people find that pennies are too much of a nuisance and end up putting them in piggy banks, dresser drawers, mayonnaise jars, and ashtrays. In effect, people just refuse to use them.

The panel says that the penny is no longer necessary in American business. If the penny were gotten rid of, prices in stores could be rounded off to the nearest nickel, sales taxes could be figured into retail prices, and the penny would no longer be needed.

"Just to replace the ones that go out of circulation is a big job. We have to produce 14 billion pennies a year. That is 78 percent of all U.S. coins minted annually," said one researcher. Professor Noah Adams, who headed an earlier study, also advised eliminating the penny. "If you look at the total cost of the coin compared to its value, it doesn't pay to make the penny," said Adams.

If the U.S. did abolish the penny, it wouldn't be the first time such a thing has happened. In 1857, production of the American half-cent was stopped because of its low value. In Norway, Brazil, and Argentina, the penny has long been discontinued.

After the 1976 study, Congress decided to change the penny's composition. Previously, pennies had been made mostly of copper. Since 1982, however, pennies have been made of 97% zinc with just a thin coating of copper. The change saved $25 million a year.

Experts continue to point out the advantages of getting rid of the penny altogether. So, why hasn't it been done yet? One argument claims that eliminating the penny would cause inflation. It would cause merchants to round prices up, not down, to the nearest nickel.

Despite all the arguments for getting rid of the penny, it seem likely that it will be around a while longer. Whenever someone proposes eliminating the penny, the nation protests. Apparently, Americans just like certain coins, and don't want change. As Webster says, "There are situations in which pennies are indispensable. When you need one, nothing else will do."

1. Why does the panel recommend getting rid of the penny?
   A. It would save money.
   B. Pennies are not that important for American business.
   C. Prices could be rounded off to a nickel.
   D. A and C are correct.
   E. A, B, and C are correct.

2. Who would make the decision to keep or eliminate pennies?
   A. the panel
   B. Noah Adams
   C. the U.S. Mint
   D. Congress
   E. people in general

3. Previously, pennies
   A. had been eliminated in 1857.
   B. cost $70 million a year.
   C. were a "nuisance to carry."
   D. caused inflation.
   E. had been made primarily of copper.

4. Pennies make up what percent of all coins?
   A. 25 million
   B. 14 billion
   C. 78
   D. one half
   E. 97

Lesson Eleven

1. **amorous** (ăm´ ər-əs) *adj.* *of or associated with love*
   He said, "Turn the lights down low and put some *amorous* music on the CD player."
   syn: lustful

2. **mammoth** (măm´ əth) *adj.* huge
   The earthquake caused *mammoth* destruction throughout China.
   syn: great size; large   *ant: tiny*

3. **devout** (dĭ-vout´) *adj.* pious; zealous
   Rita was a *devout* worshipper of God.
   syn: ardent; adoring   *ant: unholy; irreverent*

4. **garbled** (gär´ bəl) *adj.* distorted; mixed up
   Because the radio picked up two stations at once, the sound was very *garbled.*
   syn: confused; jumbled   *ant: clear*

5. **haven** (hā´ vən) *noun* place of shelter; sanctuary
   Our house became a *haven* for stray dogs.
   syn: refuge

6. **dexterity** (dĕk stĕr´ ĭ tē) *noun* skill
   The sailor showed his *dexterity* in knot tying.
   syn: expertise   *ant: clumsiness*

7. **interloper** (ĭn´ tər lō pər) *noun* intruder
   "Stop changing my work. You're like an *interloper*," yelled the author to his editor.
   syn: meddler

8. **frail** (frāl) *adj.* weak; feeble
   While Mr. Simians was over eighty, he didn't seem *frail* at all.
   syn: decrepit; unsound   *ant: solid; strong*

9. **havoc** (hăv´ ək) *noun* ruin; confusion
   The rush-hour accident caused *havoc* for returning motorists.
   syn: calamity; catastrophe

10. **sinister** (sĭ´ ĭ stər) *adj.* threatening; ominous
    The *sinister* stalker had finally been caught.
    syn: menacing   *ant: harmless; innocent*

11. **wrest** (rĕst´) *verb* to twist away from
    No one could *wrest* control of the company from its founder.
    syn: wring; extract

12. **skirmish** (skûr´ mĭsh) *noun* a small fight; a clash
    We heard the sounds of the *skirmish* as our children played army.
    syn: run-in   *ant: fierce battle*

13. **proximity** (prŏk sĭm´ĭtē) *noun* closeness
    The woodpecker used our feeder, but still stayed in close *proximity* to the trees.
    syn: nearness   *ant: distance*

14. **provincial** (prə vĭn´shəl) *adj.* rural; rustic
    The small *provincial* town had a great deal of charm for city people.
    syn: parochial   *ant: universal*

15. **sanctuary** (sāngk´chōō ĕr ē) *noun* a place of safety; haven
    While it rained, Victor found some *sanctuary* under the trees.
    syn: refuge

Exercise I — Words in Context

From the words below, supply the words needed to complete the sentences.

amorous   **mammoth**   **devoutly**   **garbled**   **haven**

A. I looked out the window and saw two _____ doves, which had obviously made a nest in one small area of our _____ barn. The tiny space they occupied was a _____ for them against all enemies. Once I heard their _____ peeps as a cat tried to climb in. As much as I like cats, though, I was _____ praying for the baby birds' safety.

From the words below, supply the words needed to complete the sentences.

dexterity   **havoc**   **interloper**   **frail**   **sinister**

B. The magician's strength and _____ astonished the audience. Then one _____ spectator stood up and exclaimed that she could escape from the locked box just as easily. The magician at once led this _____ to the stage and flashed a _____ wink to the crowd.

C. The hurricane brought _____ and destruction to the island.

From the words below, supply the words needed to complete the sentences.

wrest   **provincial**   **skirmish**   **proximity**   **sanctuary**

D. One _____ after another did little to chase the British troops from their _____ in the heavy, thick woods. The soldiers fought in close _____ to the river, which gave them the advantage over the Colonists.

E. Long battles were fought in a vain attempt to _____ the _____ capital of Philadelphia from the Americans' hands.

46

Exercise II—Analogies

Complete the analogy by choosing the most appropriate word.

1. profit: capitalism ::
   A. revenge : terrorism
   B. dictator : freedom
   C. obliteration : Nazism
   D. nonviolence : pacifism

2. pilot : bomber ::
   A. robber : safe
   B. usher : theater
   C. engineer : train
   D. emcee : quiz

3. medicine : illness ::
   A. whiskey : drunk
   B. food : famine
   C. drought : water
   D. fire : blaze

Exercise III—Roots, Prefixes, and Suffixes

What root do the following words have in common? What do you think it means?

> motorcycle
> cyclable
> cyclone
> encyclopedia

All the words use the root "cycl" which means "circle" or "wheel." In the first four, it is easy to determine the meaning, but it takes a bit of extra thought to understand its use in "encyclopedia." How do you suppose the root relates to "encyclopedia"? If you cannot figure out the answer, use a dictionary. _____

The "Cyclades" are a group of islands around another island; "cycles" recurr over a regular period. Name the monster from Greek Myths which had one round eye and who takes his name from this root. _____

Look at the suffix on the following words and determine what it means.

> outrageous
> religious
> ridiculous
> beauteous
> marvelous

The suffixes "ous," "ious," and "eous" mean "full of" or "characterized by." Many adjectives and nouns can be changed by the addition of the suffix. Examples: characterized by victory (victori-ous); like a felon (fel<u>onious</u>); full of grief (griev<u>ous</u>). In the spaces below, list some words which use the "ous" endings properly.

_____	_____	_____
_____	_____	_____

Exercise IV—Reading Comprehension ///

Read the selection and answer the questions.

The United States finds itself in the unusual and highly controversial position of being on the same side of one issue with countries whose policies it usually opposes: the imposition of the death penalty for crimes committed by a juvenile who is tried as an adult. Only Yemen, Iran, Nigeria, Pakistan, and Saudi Arabia— and the "modern" super power, America— allow such executions; however, the U.S. is the sole country which has actually done so within the recent past. To further differentiate America from other nations, China, which our government strenuously criticizes for its abuses of human rights, has abolished capital punishment for those convictions. The U.S. has signed the International Convention on Civil and Political Rights, which expressly forbids execution of juveniles, but the White House has formally lodged an exception to allow such a policy to exist.

A 26 year old man awaits lethal injection in Virginia for a murder he committed at age 17. His accomplice in the killing, a 14 year old girlfriend, was tried as a juvenile, and is now free, just as the male participant in the murder waits for death. Many doubts exist as to his sole responsibility and punishment; however, few experts expect clemency to be granted and his sentence commuted to life imprisonment. The primary reason for that belief is Virginia's record of having executed 67 people since 1977, the highest total of any state except Texas.

1. The primary purpose behind this article was probably
   A. to inform the reader.
   B. to persuade the reader.
   C. to anger the reader.
   D. to save the convict's life.
   E. to show the author's outrage.

2. Words which express an opinion, rather than inform, are:
   A. controversial, modern, and differentiate.
   B. superpower, Iran, and sole.
   C. opposes, unusual, and strenuously.
   D. responsibility, punishment, and lethal.
   E. abuses, China, and highest.

3. The author implies that the female accomplice was not sentenced to death because of
   A. her age.
   B. doubts over her participation.
   C. her sex.
   D. A and B are correct.
   E. A and C are correct.

4. The murder
   A. took place last year.
   B. was of 2 people.
   C. happened in Virginia.
   D. was committed by firearms.
   E. resulted in only one conviction.

48

1. **obscure** (ŏb-skyōōr´) *adj.* unclear; hidden
Tim knew so many tiny, *obscure* facts that he became a "Jeopardy" champion.
syn: indistinct; camouflaged   *ant: illuminated; clear*

2. **superficial** (sōō pər fĭsh´ əl) *adj.* shallow; sketchy
The mother assured the crying little girl that the cut was only *superficial*.
syn: cursory; uncritical   *ant: exhaustive; deep*

3. **tertiary** (tur´ shē ĕr ē) *adj.* of third importance
The color of the house was of *tertiary* consideration to the buyers, behind location and size.
syn: unimportant   *ant: primary*

4. **conspicuous** (kən-spĭk´ yōō əs) *adj.* obvious; clear
We looked out of place and *conspicuous* in tuxedos.
syn: noticeable; showy   *ant: hidden; ordinary*

5. **nullify** (nŭl´ ə-fī) *verb* to abolish; negate
Do not *nullify* your fine words with thoughtless behavior.
syn: neutralize

6. **retort** (rĭ tôrt´) *noun* reply; rejoinder
The stand-up comedian had a hilarious *retort* for every heckler.
syn: answer; wisecrack

7. **reverberate** (rĭ vûr´ bə rāt) *verb* to echo
Tarzan's loud call *reverberated* through the jungle.
syn: to resound

8. **permeate** (pûr´ mē-āt) *verb* to penetrate; to spread or flow throughout.
Environmentalists warned that foreign plants had *permeated* our state.
syn: to pervade

9. **jubilant** (jōō´ bə lənt) *adj.* joyous; happy
The *jubilant* lottery winner soon spent her money unwisely.
syn: overjoyed   *ant: depressed; unhappy*

10. **concise** (kən sīs´) *adj.* short; brief
Many times a *concise* answer is preferable to a long, involved one.
syn: succinct   *ant: redundant; wordy*

11. **disparage** (dĭ spar´ ĭ j) *verb* to belittle; to abuse
The unethical stock broker *disparaged* the stock even as he was buying it himself.
syn: to detract from; to denigrate   *ant: to compliment*

12. **ethics** (ĕth´ ĭks) *noun* morals; principles
Ethics is a way to teach a person right and wrong.
syn: standards; ideals

13. **irrelevant** (ĭ rĕl´ ə vənt) *adj.* not pertinent
I thought that Shakespeare was *irrelevant* to my chosen area of study.
syn: immaterial; inapplicable   *ant: relevant; germane*

14. **authoritarian** (ə thôr ĭ târ´ ē ən) *adj.* dictatorial; strict
It is easier to work for an understanding boss, rather than one who is *authoritarian.*
syn: totalitarian   *ant: democratic*

15. **malnutrition** (mal nōō-trĭ sh´ ən) *noun* lack of healthy nutrition
It seems to make no sense, but *malnutrition* frequently makes the stomach swell.

Exercise I — Words in Context //

From the words below, supply the words needed to complete the sentences.

obscure	**superficial**	**tertiary**	**conspicuously**	**nullify**

A.   The treaty was simple to _____, because neither party had put much thought into the _____ details. One idea, which had been thought to be extremely significant, proved to be of _____ importance, behind two others. Another paragraph was so _____ that no one understood it completely. The main concept supposedly in the agreement, however, was _____ absent.

From the words below, supply the words needed to complete the sentences.

retorted	**reverberated**	**permeated**	**jubilant**	**concise**

B.   The newest rock hit _____ from radios everywhere. The song was so infectious and _____ , it seemed as though every teenager, and most parents, listened to it. The song_____ almost all radio stations in the area. One group, however, dissented and issued a _____ statement claiming the song was filled with hidden meanings. The band _____ that the accusation was "nonsense."

From the words below, supply the words needed to complete the sentences.

disparaged	**ethics**	**irrelevant**	**malnutrition**	**authoritarian**

C.   Even though business _____ was taught in the college, most students thought the course was _____ to their lives. They _____ the professor as too strict and _____ for such a course.

D.   Many died of _____ during the famine.

Exercise II—Analogies

Complete the analogy by choosing the most appropriate word.

1. downpour : flood ::
   A. lunar : eclipse
   B. snowfall : blizzard
   C. tornado : wind
   D. cyclone : hurricane

2. inconsequential : vital ::
   A. mortal : deceased
   B. flammable : combustible
   C. infinite : void
   D. negative : positive

3. listless : energetic ::
   A. lurid : sensational
   B. indigent : weak
   C. despondent : hopeful
   D. sordid : responsive

Exercise III—Roots, Prefixes, and Suffixes

In this lesson, we have included two closely related prefixes. Look at the list and see if you can determine the meaning of the prefixes.

intercept	intrastate	interstellar
intravenous	interaction	intracoastal
intercontinental	interior	

The prefix "inter" means "between," "among," "in the middle of," or "during." The prefix "intra," however, means only "within." Answer the following questions:

A. Does your school have "intermural" or "intramural" sports?
B. Does a California "intrastate" bus go to Nevada?
C. Do you receive an "intravenous" injection before an operation?
D. Does a reporter conduct an "intraview"?
E. Why wouldn't primitive tribes engage in "intratribal" raids?
F. If a football player "intracepts" a pass, where would he find himself?

A. _____
B. _____
C. _____
D. _____
E. _____
F. _____

Exercise IV—Reading Comprehension

Read the selection and answer the questions.

In his book Mr. Harris explains that the choice of what foods are acceptable to eat within any society is determined by questions of supply and demand. He explains that those foods considered good to eat in any culture are those foods that have a more favorable balance of practical benefits over costs. Those foods considered bad to eat, though, have a high direct or indirect cost attached to them.

Harris offered the following example to explain his point. The reason Hindus in India do not eat cows is not that their religion forbids it. Rather, Hinduism has adopted the most sensible eating habits,

51

given the economics of India. Cattle in India are cheap, and the poor people use them for plowing, and they drink their milk. They also burn their manure for heat. If Indians began to eat beef, the price of cattle would rise. These poor people would no longer be able to use them. In a short time, the society would collapse.

Another example is the practice of eating the flesh of horses. Horses have never been raised for meat nor milk in the United States mainly because other animals such as cattle, pigs, and sheep, are plentiful and less costly to raise. Also, the horse's usefulness as a beast of labor, as well as the practice of horse racing, have led Americans to look on the horse as a sort of pet. To most Americans, the idea of eating a horse is disgusting. This exists, despite the popularity of the common expression, "hungry enough to eat a horse."

Europeans do not share that feeling. After the French Revolution when the poor people rose up against the rich, the idea of the horse as a noble animal that should be protected was destroyed. The peasants saw the horse as a symbol of the rich they hated. They have been eating horses ever since.

1. According to the author, what determines a society's food preferences?
    A. religion
    B. taste
    C. use and supply
    D. cultural practices
    E. supply and demand

2. If the poor of India began to eat beef, the author believes
    A. the price would rise.
    B. Indian society might crumble.
    C. horses would replace cows.
    D. A and B are correct.
    E. A, B, and C are correct.

3. One reason Americans do not eat horses is that
    A. horses are shown in movies.
    B. we consider the horse dirty.
    C. we view horses as noble.
    D. horses are considered pets.
    E. Europeans eat them.

4. Horses were originally eaten in Europe
    A. during famines.
    B. because of their abundance.
    C. because the horse represented nobility.
    D. because they were a good source of meat.
    E. because they had so many other uses.

Lesson Thirteen

1. **exonerate** (ĭg-zŏn´ə-rāt) *verb* to clear of wrongdoing
   DNA evidence was enough to completely *exonerate* the accused.
   syn: to absolve; to acquit   *ant: to incriminate*

2. **fabricate** (fab´rĭ-kāt) *verb* to make up; to construct
   Each time the little boy *fabricated* another lie to explain the previous lie, his parents became angrier.
   syn: to devise; to concoct

3. **bizarre** (bĭ-zär´) *adj.* strange; fantastic
   The roller coaster made some *bizarre*, unexpected twists.
   syn: unusual; weird   *ant: ordinary; regular*

4. **placate** (plā´ kāt) *verb* to calm; to pacify
   No one could *placate* the grieving widow.
   syn: to assuage; to tranquilize   *ant: to enrage; to anger*

5. **unabated** (ən ə-bāt´ ĕd) *adj.* unceasing; with undiminished force
   The Bible says that Noah saw the rain fall in an *unabated* fashion for 40 days.
   syn: never-ending   *ant: lessened*

6. **sedate** (sĭ-dāt´) *verb* to tranquilize; to compose
   In order to operate on the horse they *sedated* it.
   syn: to calm   *ant: to agitate*

7. **precipitation** (prĭ-sĭp ĭ-tā´ shən) *noun* rain, snow, or hail
   Precipitation, in the form of snow, blanketed the area.

8. **dubious** (dōō´ bē əs) *adj.* doubtful; arguable
   His claim to the money seemed *dubious* to the judge.
   syn: improbable; unlikely   *ant: reliable*

9. **venomous** (vĕn´ ə-məs) *adj.* poisonous
   Bill was such a cynic that he had a *venomous* remark handy at all times.
   syn: toxic   *ant: harmless*

10. **elapse** (ĭ-laps´) *verb* to pass
    Barely an hour had *elapsed* before the crook was caught.
    syn: to run out; pass

11. **bristle** (brĭs´ əl) *verb* to anger; to rage
    I *bristled* with anger when he insulted my ancestry.
    syn: to fume; to seethe   *ant: to calm*

12. **construe** (kən-strōō´) *verb* to explain; to interpret a meaning
The band *construed* our silence as approval, but it was really boredom.
syn: to spell out; interpret

13. **oratory** (ôr´ ə-tôr ē) *noun* speech
Jane showed her expertise at debate and *oratory*.
syn: elocution; rhetoric

14. **implore** (ĭm-plôr´) *verb* to beg; to appeal to
I *implored* my ex-friend to treat me fairly.
syn: to plead

15. **inhibition** (ĭn hə-bĭsh´ ən) *noun* restraint; hindrance
The driver showed no *inhibitions* about passing the police car.
syn: prohibition

Exercise I — Words in Context

From the words below, supply the words needed to complete the sentences.

exonerate	fabricated	bizarre	placate	unabated

A. Lawyers worked day and night, _____, to prevent their client's execution on what they claimed were _____ charges. The crime had involved murder with a _____ type of poison. The attorneys had worked for an entire year to _____ the man wrongly accused. The public, however, differed and in order to _____ those demanding death, the prisoner was kept out of sight.

From the words below, supply the words needed to complete the sentences.

sedated	precipitated	dubious	venomous	elapsed

B. I was sure the snake was not _____ , but when it bit me, that belief became highly _____ . In the hospital after two hours had _____ , and I was in horrible pain, the doctor _____ me and operated. I eventually recovered, but that one incident _____ my fear of snakes.

From the words below, supply the words needed to complete the sentences.

bristled	construed	oratory	implored	inhibitions

C. Mr. Jones' venom-filled _____ inflamed the people in the audience. They _____ at each racist remark and began to push forward. The police _____ him to cease and desist from continuing his speech. Jones, however, _____ the warning as prohibiting his free speech and declared that he had never felt any _____ when stating his opinions.

Exercise II—Analogies ///

Complete the analogy by choosing the most appropriate word.

1. mountain : climb ::
   A. window : break
   B. baseball : hit
   C. dictionary : discuss
   D. communication : speak

2. laboratory : microscope ::
   A. brick : mortar
   B. food : dessert
   C. chicken : egg
   D. home : bathroom

3. clemency : pardon ::
   A. fret : worry
   B. lurid : cheap
   C. irk : like
   D. culprit : guilt

Exercise III—Roots, Prefixes, and Suffixes ///

Next, we have two suffixes which have opposite meanings. The first is a common one. The second is less well-known but just as important. Here is a list of words containing both. See if you recognize any of them and can figure out what the suffixes mean.

hydrophobia	hemophiliac
claustrophobic	bibliophile
arachnophobia	Anglophile

You probable have been able to determine that "phobia" means "fear of," and "phobic" refers to a person with a fear; "phile" means a "preference for" and "philiac" is a person who has that preference.

The roots of the words are also useful.

biblio	=	book
hydro	=	water
claustro	=	closed in
arachne	=	spider
hemo	=	blood
Anglo	=	English

Now that you know both root and suffix, define the six words.

A.   hydrophobia   _____

B.   hemophiliac   _____

C.   claustrophobia   _____

D.   bibliophile   _____

E.   Anglophile   _____

F.   arachnophobia   _____

Exercise IV—Reading Comprehension ///

Read the selection and answer the questions.

Rabies is a disease carried by animals. It is a deadly disease, and any human or animal bitten by a rabid animal is likely to die if treatment is not provided. As early as 2000 B.C. the Greeks recognized that a mad dog, bitten by another mad dog, becomes mad itself.

While rabies had been common in Europe for a long time, most experts think the disease was brought to America during Colonial times. The first case of a mad or rabid dog was reported in Virginia in 1753. It is believed that the dog had been brought from England. Shortly after this, rabies was found in foxes and skunks.

It was not until 1953, however, that rabid raccoons began to appear in Florida. While the first cases were no cause for alarm, it soon became clear that a problem was developing. Like a stain from a spilled soda, the rabid raccoons spread through Georgia, Virginia, West Virginia, and Maryland. By 1988, rabid raccoons were also found in Pennsylvania, Delaware, and the District of Columbia.

But not only are there more cases of rabid raccoons, there are also more reports of rabid cats and dogs. This, of course, makes the danger to humans greater. Humans are more likely to be bitten by a rabid dog or cat, than they are likely to be bitten by a rabid raccoon. In fact, there are almost no cases reported of humans having been bitten by raccoons. This may be because most people have the good sense to stay far away from a sick or tame-appearing wild animal. But every once in a while some misguided person will "rescue" a young wild raccoon. In bringing this kind of animal home, in touching it even, the person risks exposing himself and others to this deadly disease. While it is true that humans can be treated if bitten by a rabid animal, the treatments are not always 100% successful, and the treatments are always very painful.

In addition to staying away from "wild" animals, experts warn that you should get your dog or cat vaccinated with a rabies shot. If bitten by any animal, wash the wound thoroughly and see a doctor.

1. The best title for this article might be
    A. Rapid Response Prevents Rabies.
    B. A Short History of Rabies.
    C. Rabies Spreads in U.S.
    D. Rabies, Raccoons, and Humans.
    E. The Bite that Kills.

2. Rabies was first discovered in raccoons in the U.S. in
    A. 1753.
    B. 1953.
    C. Georgia.
    D. 1988.
    E. The 19th Century.

3. Which of the following is *not* written or implied in the article?
    A. Most rabies bites are not from raccoons.
    B. Raccoons can give rabies to different kinds of animals.
    C. Treatment for rabies is painful.
    D. Any animal can carry rabies.
    E. A mad dog will foam at the mouth.

4. According to the article, rabies
    A. usually kills if untreated.
    B. began in ancient Greek times.
    C. is only caused by animal bites.
    D. spread throughout the U.S. before the 20th Century.
    E. is also called hydrophobia.

Lesson Fourteen

1. **fret** (frĕt´) *verb* to worry
   The millionaire constantly *fretted* over his investments.

2. **malady** (măl´ə dē) *noun* illness; ailment
   Many *maladies* are preventable by simple cleanliness.
   syn: sickness

3. **listless** (lĭst´ lĭs) *adj.* spiritless; uninterested
   The injured, *listless* puppy cried pitifully.
   syn: lackadaisical; indifferent   *ant: active; eager*

4. **insurgent** (ĭn-sûr´ jənt) *noun* one who revolts
   Most *insurgents* eventually become violent revolutionaries.
   syn: rebel

5. **whet** (wĕt) *verb* to sharpen
   The smell of steak cooking just *whetted* my appetite.
   syn: to awaken; to hone   *ant: to dull*

6. **morose** (mə rōs´) *adj.* sad
   The cat ran away, and its owner was *morose* until it returned.
   syn: gloomy   *ant: happy*

7. **remote** (rē mōt´) *adj.* distant
   Borneo is such a *remote* island that it gets few visitors.
   syn: far off   *ant: close*

8. **tinged** (tĭnjd) *adj.* tinted
   The dress was *tinged* with green.
   syn: colored

9. **hypothetical** (hī pə thĕt´ ĭ kəl) *adj.* assumed
   Hypothetical questions begin with "if" and are extremely tricky.
   syn: supposed   *ant: genuine*

10. **brash** (brăsh) *adj.* impulsive; hasty
    His *brash* tone of voice surprised us, since he was usually so polite.
    syn: rash   *ant: polite*

11. **prelude** (prəl´ yōōd) *noun* preface
    The "Star Spangled Banner" is played as a *prelude* to sporting events.
    syn: beginning   *ant: finish*

12. **preclude** (prĭ klōōd´) *verb* to prevent
A criminal record will *preclude* your becoming a teacher.
syn: to eliminate   *ant: to allow*

13. **subordinate** (sə bôr´ dn ĭt) *adj.* of less importance
The *subordinate* conjunction was punctuated incorrectly.
syn: inferior; secondary   *ant: superior*

14. **arbitrary** (är´ bĭ trĕr ē) *adj.* indiscriminate; impetuous
The judge's decision was so *arbitrary* that we appealed it.
syn: erratic; unreasonable   *ant: definite; legitimate*

15. **doleful** (dōl´ fəl) *adj.* sad; sorrowful
Her sad, *doleful* look told us she wouldn't be graduating with her class.
syn: miserable; wretched   *ant: cheerful*

Exercise I — Words in Context

From the words below, supply the words needed to complete the sentences.

fret	**malady**	**listless**	**insurgent**	**whet**

A. After the _____ force was easily defeated, the victorious soldiers, rather than becoming more enthusiastic, were tired and _____.

B. "Don't _____," said the security guard to the lost child.

C. The carpenter had to _____ the chisel before using it.

D. One _____ after another forced Bob into the hospital.

From the words below, supply the words needed to complete the sentences.

morose	**remote**	**tinge**	**hypothetical**	**brash**

E. When she realized there was not even a _____ chance of making up with her friends, Roberta became sad, then _____, and finally depressed.

F. At his news conference, the President answered a _____ question from the reporter with more than a _____ of sarcasm.

G. The _____ young boy was frequently punished.

From the words below, supply the words needed to complete the sentences.

prelude   **preclude**   **subordinates**   **arbitrary**   **doleful**

H.   In order to _____ a long strike, the manager offered a(n) _____ pay raise of $1.00 an hour.

I.   Although the general usually treated his _____ kindly, he lashed out at them if they made a mistake.

J.   As a _____ to the main course, we have soup.

K.   A long _____ moan from the monster frightened the audience.

Exercise II—Analogies //

Complete the analogy by choosing the most appropriate word.

1. imperturbable : unshakable ::
    A.   immaterial : relevant
    B.   malady : illness
    C.   garbled : clear
    D.   engrossed : bothered

2. feather : peacock ::
    A.   mane : lion
    B.   radio : car
    C.   tail : elephant
    D.   figure : computer

3. condolence : sympathy ::
    A.   opaque : clarity
    B.   compile : erect
    C.   aspirant : completion
    D.   carousel : merry-go-round

Exercise III—Roots, Prefixes, and Suffixes //

Look back at the previous lesson, if you need to, in order to define the following words, or use the dictionary.

A.   bibliography   _____

B.   hydrosphere   _____

C.   hemotoxin   _____

D.   Anglo-French   _____

E.   arachnid   _____

F.   hydrometer   _____

G   Bible   _____

H.   hydrodynamics   _____

I.   Anglican   _____

J   hydroelectric   _____

K.   hemostat   _____

Read the selection and answer the questions.

There's a race of men that don't fit in,
  A race that can't stay still;
So they break the hearts of kith and kin,
  And they roam the world at will.
They range the field and they rove the flood,
  And they climb the mountain's crest;
Theirs is the curse of the gypsy blood,
  And they don't know how to rest.

If they just went straight they might go far;
  They are strong and brave and true;
But they're always tired of the things that are,
  And they want the strange and new.
They say: "Could I find my proper groove,
  What a deep mark I would make!"
So they chop and change, and each fresh move
  Is only a fresh mistake.

And each forgets, as he strips and runs
  With a brilliant, fitful pace,
It's the steady, quiet, plodding ones
  Who win in the lifelong race.
And each forgets that his youth has fled,
  Forgets that his prime is past,
Till he stands one day, with a hope that's dead,
  In the glare of the truth at last.

He has failed, he has failed; he has missed his
      chance;
  He has just done things by half.
Life's been a jolly good joke on him,
  And now is the time to laugh.
Ha, ha! He is one of the Legion Lost;
  He was never meant to win;
He's a rolling stone, and it's bred in the bone;
  He's a man who won't fit in.

Author: Robert Service

1.   The best title for this poem would be
    A.   Gypsy Blood.
    B.   A Rolling Stone.
    C.   The Men That Don't Fit In.
    D.   Stay Put and Prosper.
    E.   Lost Legions Lose.

2.   In stanza 1 the word "race" means
    A.   contest.
    B.   ethnic group.
    C.   particular type.
    D.   onward movement.
    E.   all the above are correct.

3.   The best re-stating of the point of the poem is
    A.   constant change brings happiness.
    B.   people desiring new places to live will never find them.
    C.   it is better to wander than stay still.
    D.   those who continually seek new experiences will only be unhappy.
    E.   life passes you by, if you don't try new experiences.

4.   According to the poem, people who wander the world
    A.   suffer from a curse.
    B.   believe in their abilities.
    C.   cannot be satisfied.
    D.   are overtaken by steady, direct ones.
    E.   all the above are correct.

Lesson Fifteen

1. **incoherent** (ĭn kō hîr´ ənt) *adj.* unclear; disjointed
   When in shock, he mumbled in an *incoherent* way about his grandfather.
   syn: muddled; disorganized   *ant: orderly; clear*

2. **falter** (fôl´ tər) *verb* to hesitate; to halt
   Terrible weather caused the expedition to *falter* in its quest.
   syn: to waver   *ant: to persevere*

3. **irate** (ī rāt´) *adj.* angry
   He called the Better Business Bureau because he was *irate* at being swindled.
   syn: mad   *ant: happy*

4. **painstaking** (pānz´ tā kĭng) *adj.* careful; conscientious
   His recovery from the dreadful accident was long and *painstaking*.
   syn: meticulous   *ant: careless*

5. **reprehensible** (rĕp rĭ hĕn´ sə bəl) *adj.* deserving of rebuke
   I believe that lying is more *reprehensible* than stealing.
   syn: blameworthy   *ant: praiseworthy*

6. **restrictive** (rĭ strĭk´ tĭv) *adj.* limiting
   Our curfew felt more *restrictive* than it actually was.
   syn: narrowed

7. **convalesce** (kŏn´ və lĕs) *verb* to recover
   Tom had a long period to *convalesce* after the car hit him.
   syn: to improve; to recuperate   *ant: to deteriorate*

8. **octogenarian** (ŏk tə jə nâr´ ē ən) *noun* someone between 80 and 89 years old
   Many *octogenarians* are still alert and active.

9. **fitful** (fĭt´ fəl) *adj.* intermittent; sporadic
   Nightmares made for a *fitful* night's sleep.
   syn: interrupted; irregular   *ant: constant*

10. **stereotype** (stĕr ē ə tĭp´ ĭ kl) *noun* cliché; an oversimplified concept or image
    The *stereotype* of a pitbull is a dog which is always mean and dangerous.
    syn: a set form; generalization

11. **respite** (rĕs´ pĭt) *noun* rest; break
    They needed a *respite* from work and went on a vacation.
    syn: time-out; reprieve

12. **stagnate** (stag´nāt) *verb* to stop developing
If you let your children sit in front of television all day, they will *stagnate*.
syn: to become sluggish and dull

13. **ascend** (ə sĕnd´) *verb* to climb
The old man took the elevator rather than try to *ascend* by the steps.
syn: to mount   *ant: to descend*

14. **dregs** (drĕgs) *noun* the least valuable part
Most people have little use for those who they view as the *dregs* of society.
syn: lowest element   *ant: pinnacle*

15. **intemperate** (ĭn tĕm´pər ĭt) *adj.* unwise; excessive
Making *intemperate* comments about Stalin in Russia meant certain imprisonment.
syn: unrestrained; passionate   *ant: carefully considered; thought out*

Exercise I — Words in Context

From the words below, supply the words needed to complete the sentences.

incoherent	falter	irate	painstaking	reprehensible

A.   "You speak like a(n) _____ drunk," said the officer to the suspect. "Stealing from the church wasn't only dumb, but also _____.

B.   The tightrope walker did not _____ when his long pole fell; completing the act without it, however, proved to be _____ work.

C.   I was _____ at the ticket price for the show, but went anyway.

From the words below, supply the words needed to complete the sentences.

restrictive	convalescence	octogenarian	fitful	stereotype

D.   When the _____ night had passed, the wrinkled _____ demanded that the nurse at the hospital remove his _____ bandaging at once. The old man was not the typical _____ of a weak, frail 85 year old.

E.   A long _____ is needed when you break a bone.

From the words below, supply the words needed to complete the sentences.

respite	stagnate	ascend	dregs	intemperate

F.   "Cease your _____ remarks to this court immediately," said the judge, "or I'll send you to a jail cell until you_____."

G.   While the tourist was determined to _____ the lighthouse, he looked for any moment of_____ from the task.

H.   Wine is usually missing the _____ at the bottom if it has been strained.

62

Exercise II—Analogies

Complete the analogy by choosing the most appropriate word.

1. flamboyant : gaudy ::
   A. jubilant : expressive
   B. convalesce: recover
   C. listless : irrelevant
   D. brazen : humble

2. upset : irate ::
   A. poor : wealthy
   B. accost : assault
   C. harass : befriend
   D. brash : opulent

3. chapter : novel ::
   A. congregation : worship
   B. school : pupil
   C. window : pane
   D. cow : herd

Exercise III—Roots, Prefixes, and Suffixes

Place these words with prefixes that refer to numbers in the correct numerical order.

A.	binomial	1. _____
B.	decade	2. _____
C.	octagon	3. _____
D.	triangle	4. _____
E.	unicycle	5. _____
F.	quintet	6. _____
G.	nonagenarian	7. _____
H.	quadruplets	8. _____
I.	sextuplets	9. _____
J.	septennial	10. _____

Congratulations! You have just counted from 1-10 using Latin prefixes. See if you can do it again, this time using your own words with the proper prefixes. A word for "9" might be difficult to find, though.

1. _____   6. _____
2. _____   7. _____
3. _____   8. _____
4. _____   9. _____
5. _____   10. _____

Exercise IV—Reading Comprehension

Read the selection and answer the questions.

Paul Burbutis, a professor of entomology at the University of Delaware, has spent 15 years seeking a way to control one of the world's most destructive agricultural pests, the corn borer. Now, he has found a small black wasp which he thinks might do the job.

"The corn borer is a small, flesh-colored caterpillar about an inch long," said Dr. Burbutis. "It causes between 1 million and 2 million dollars worth of damage on Delaware corn farms each year. We can control it with heavy coatings of insecticides, but that gets very expensive. As you know, insecticides are also bad for the environment."

Dr. Burbutis explained that the corn borer got its name because the young insects bore their way into the base of the ears of corn. Once there, they form cocoons. They then emerge from the cocoons about a week later as fully grown moths.

The black wasp that Dr. Burbutis is working with is a natural enemy of corn borers. "The wasps are so small that 25 could fit on the head of a pin," said Dr. Burbutis. "The female lays its eggs inside the corn borer's eggs. Then the young wasp eats the inside out of the borer's egg and spins a cocoon. In effect it makes the corn borer's egg its own home." Naturally, this destroys the corn borer.

Dr. Burbutis hopes someday to be able to breed the black wasps by the hundreds of millions in factories. This would result in the making of a living insecticide. The wasps could then be sprayed on fields, just as an insecticide is. Unfortunately, the only way to breed the wasps at present is to breed large amounts of borer eggs. The wasps eat nothing else. "We're trying to come up with a method to artificially duplicate the borer eggs. But more research needs to be done," said Dr. Burbutis.

Scientists don't expect the wasps to entirely wipe out the corn borer population even if they do find a way to breed the wasps in large numbers. For one thing, other insects eat the wasps themselves. One such insect is the common ladybug. But scientists do see the wasp as one part of a total plan.

Another enemy of the corn corer is the disgusting Lydella Thompsoni fly. This insect bears its young outside the holes of corn borers. "The young flies burrow into the bodies of the borers. There they live like maggots, until they are ready to crawl out and become adult flies," said Dr. Burbutis. "By then, the borers are no more." Scientists made an attempt to control borers in the 1940's by releasing millions of the Lydella flies. But for some unknown reason, the flies had disappeared by 1958. Years later, another attempt to establish them was begun, but thus far the results are not known.

1. The best title for this selection is
   A. Insect Pests.
   B. Control of Corn Borers.
   C. New Attempt at Pest Control.
   D. A Living Insecticide.
   E. Dr. Burbutis' Experiments.

2. The corn borer
   A. is extremely small.
   B. gets its name from where its young live.
   C. causes over $2 million in crop damage.
   D. will be eliminated by wasps.
   E. All the above are correct.

3. The wasps and flies described in the article
   A. both eat the mature corn borer.
   B. are attempts to control the corn borer.
   C. are easily bred.
   D. get eaten by ladybugs.
   E. A and B are correct.

4. Lydella Thompsoni flies
   A. were released previously, but disappeared.
   B. are ineffective in controlling corn borers.
   C. are an expensive method of pest control.
   D. were discovered by Dr. Burbutis.
   E. kill corn borers the same way as the black fly does.

Lesson Sixteen

1. **rampart** (răm´ pərt) *noun* a defensive structure
   A dozen enemy troops stormed the castle *ramparts*.
   syn: stronghold; bulwark

2. **retract** (rĭ trăkt´) *verb* to pull back or in
   I saw Fluffy the cat *retract* her claws just after she was done scratching the couch.
   syn: to withdraw   *ant: to project*

3. **pittance** (pĭt´ ns) *noun* small amount
   He had to get a new job because he had only a *pittance* left in his account.
   syn: trace; smidgen   *ant: abundance*

4. **eminent** (ĕm´ ə nənt) *adj.* famous; prominent
   The *eminent* politician delivered the commencement address at graduation.
   syn: renowned; famed   *ant: unknown; common*

5. **interrogate** (ĭn tĕr´ ə gāt) *verb* to question
   Shortly after his transfer, the prisoner was brutally *interrogated* for six hours.
   syn: to quiz

6. **exploits** (ĕk´ sploit) *noun* adventures; achievements
   The travel book chronicles the brave *exploits* of people in primitive places.
   syn: feats

7. **kindle** (kĭnd´ l) *verb* to light
   Even though Robert had not seen Camellia for twenty years, the sight of her *rekindled* all the old feelings.
   syn: to ignite   *ant: to extinguish*

8. **clemency** (klĕm´ ən sē) *noun* mercy; leniency
   The governor granted the convicted murderer *clemency* just prior to her execution.
   syn: forgiveness   *ant: harshness*

9. **pragmatic** (prăg măt´ ĭk) *adj.* practical; down-to-earth
   He is a *pragmatic* person who knows how to get the job done.
   syn: realistic   *ant: idealistic*

10. **writhe** (rīth) *verb* to twist; to wriggle
    The kite's long tail *writhed* about as if it were a real serpent.
    syn: to squirm

11. **articulate** (är tĭk´ yə lĭt) *adj.* well-spoken; clear
    He was one of our most *articulate* Presidents, one who could clearly explain complicated problems.
    syn: clear, distinct manner of speaking; eloquent   *ant: inarticulate; unintelligible*

12. **cant** (kănt) *noun* language; vocabulary
Juan changed his major from philosophy because he could no longer understand the *cant* of his professor.
syn: terminology

13. **immaterial** (ĭm mə tîr´ ē əl) *adj.* irrelevant; not pertaining
The judge ruled that the girlfriend's testimony was *immaterial*, and the case was quickly lost.
syn: not related to the subject; unsubstantial   *ant: material*

14. **wince** (wĭns) *verb* to flinch
The doctor noticed that his patients seemed to *wince* during their injections.
syn: cringe

15. **talon** (tăl´ ən) *noun* claw
We could see that the small animal could not escape the eagle's *talons*.

Exercise I — Words in Context

From the words below, supply the words needed to complete the sentences.

rampart	retract	pittance	eminent	interrogate

A.   Although he was guilty as charged, the _____ politician refused to let the police _____ him yet, for fear he would say something he later would be forced to _____.

B.   Only a _____ existed in the Royal Treasury, so the Queen decided to tax her subjects more in order to build another _____ on her castle.

From the words below, supply the words needed to complete the sentences.

exploits	kindle	clemency	pragmatic	writhed

C.   It was nearly impossible for the cub scout to re_____ the fire.

D.   I prefer _____ results, rather than just _____for their own sake.

E.   The _____ board refused to hear the murderer's appeal.

F.   The quarterback _____ in agony with a broken leg.

From the words below, supply the words needed to complete the sentences.

articulate	cant	immaterial	wince	talon

G.   After the fight, blood oozed from the bird's wounded _____.

H.   He had difficulty trying to _____ his desires to the psychiatrist, even though they were_____to his illness.

I.   Although Alicia was an atheist, she tried not to _____ when her religion teacher talked about the Bible. Alicia believed none of that _____ any more.

66

Exercise II—Analogies

Complete the analogy by choosing the most appropriate word.

1. keyboard : monitor ::
   A. muscle : organ
   B. drape : curtain
   C. fish : shark
   D. test : grade

2. violin : orchestra ::
   A. key : lock
   B. hand : watch
   C. television : remote
   D. dollar : coin

3. specific : definite ::
   A. commonplace : ordinary
   B. calculation : answer
   C. banal : important
   D. urban : rural

Exercise III—Roots, Prefixes, and Suffixes

The roots "vit' and "viv" both mean to live. They are used in words such as:

survive	revive	vital
vivisection	revitalized	vivid

Place the above words properly in these sentences.

A. I have a _____ memory of the horrible _____ of a frog performed in biology class.
B. In order to _____, I gathered all the _____ equipment.
C. The water had _____ our strength; we crossed the desert with _____ energy.

Exercise IV—Reading Comprehension

Read the selection and answer the questions.

Turpan, China, is one of the hottest and driest towns in the world. In mid-summer, the air temperature ranges from 104 to 120 degrees. But the temperature of the ground can rise even higher than that. At times it goes above 170 degrees. Less that half an inch of rain falls on the area in a year. Most of the rain that falls evaporates before it hits the ground. Yet, despite these terrible conditions, Turpan grows some of the finest melons, grapes, and cotton in the world. In so doing, it supports a population of 186,000 people.

Turpan's secret is a 2000 year old system of underground wells and tunnels. These tunnels extend over a combined distance of 1000 miles under the desert floor. This irrigation system is called the "karez." The entire system collects water which flows down from melting icecaps on top of the Tien Shan mountains.

As ice melts on top of the mountains, water flows downward through a series of wells towards the valley. If it flowed along the blazing hot desert surface, it would evaporate. But the temperature in the underground canals is low enough to prevent this from happening. Mohammed Liu explains that work on the karez was begun about 2000 years ago. "The first wells were dug out by hand," he explained. "Most of those built centuries ago are still in use."

The karez is not the only way in which the people of the area have fought the desert climate. Every house in Turpan has a basement beneath it. It is here people go to escape the mid-day heat. After the sun goes down, they come out to sleep on the flat rooftops. Here they can catch whatever breezes might be stirring.

As successful as it is, work on the karez continues. "We are reinforcing the tunnels with concrete pipe," said Liu. "Now they should last another 2000 years. We are also surrounding the fields and vineyards with 10,000 acres of trees and brush. The trees and bushes will protect the crops from sandstorms."

Turpan today stands as an example of man's determination to find a way to survive in the most unlikely places; places such as Turpan, where man must deal with heat, sandstorms, and dryness, stand as monuments to man's strength, brains, and determination.

1. The best title for the article is
   A. Life in Turpan.
   B. Melons Sustain Life in Desert.
   C. Survival Amid Adversity.
   D. How to Live in the Desert.
   E. Liu Explains Turpan.

2. What happens to most of the rain that actually does fall in and around Turpan?
   A. It is collected in wells.
   B. It evaporates.
   C. It falls on the mountains.
   D. The article does not explain.
   E. A and C are correct.

3. The karez
   A. extends for more than 2000 miles.
   B. is a series of mountains.
   C. was dug to irrigate Turpan's crops.
   D. needs protection from the sandstorms.
   E. is a system of cooling units.

4. It can be assumed that Liu
   A. is an architect.
   B. is a town official.
   C. helped build the karez.
   D. works underground.
   E. None of the above are correct.

Lesson Seventeen

1. **engrossed** (ĕn grōsd´) *adj.* deeply involved; occupied
   Once he became *engrossed* in a book, few things interrupted him.
   syn: absorbed   *ant: distracted*

2. **improvise** (ĭm´ prə vīz) *verb* to make up on the spot
   If he didn't know the answer, Michael often *improvised* one.
   syn: to extemporize

3. **shun** (shŭn) *verb* to reject; to snub
   According to some religious beliefs, members must *shun* outsiders.
   syn: to scorn; to avoid   *ant: to accept; to welcome*

4. **subterranean** (sŭb tə rā´ nē ən) *adj.* underground
   White alligators are rumored to live in the *subterranean* sewer system of New York.

5. **profound** (prə found´) *adj.* major; deep
   Although the twins were identical, they exhibited *profound* personality differences.
   syn: intense

6. **regatta** (rĭ gä´ tə) *noun* boat race
   Almost anyone with a boat entered the *regatta* held each summer.

7. **viable** (vī´ ə bəl) *adj.* capable of living
   No one thought the tree that was struck by lightning would survive, but it was quite *viable*.
   syn: living   *ant: dead*

8. **rail** (rāl) *verb* to complain bitterly
   The farmer *railed* and yelled to the heavens about the flood that destroyed his crop.
   syn: to shriek

9. **impunity** (ĭm pyōō´ nĭ tē) *noun* exemption from punishment
   The thief kept stealing with *impunity* as if he would never be caught.
   syn: immunity   *ant: culpability*

10. **prodigy** (prŏd´ ə jē) *noun* phenomenon
    The musical competition was won by an older conductor, not by the child *prodigy*.
    syn: marvel

11. **aspirant** (ăs´ pər ənt) *noun* candidate
    Only one *aspirant* for the class drama production showed up.
    syn: applicant

12. **flamboyant** (flăm boi´ ənt) *adj.* showy; ostentatious
    Ford introduced a line of *flamboyant* colors in its new models.
    syn: flashy; garish   *ant: plain; simple*

13. **indigent** (ĭn´dĭ jĭnt) *adj.* poor, destitute
Many *indigent* men lined up, hoping to be hired for the few available jobs.
syn: penniless   *ant: affluent*

14. **opportune** (ŏp ər tōōn´) *adj.* favorable; suitable
Since his weakened condition had passed, Brad chose an *opportune* moment to leave the hospital.
syn: fortunate

15. **succumb** (sə kŭmd´) *verb* to yield; to submit
After weeks of constant bombing, the enemy finally *succumbed* to our overwhelming force.
syn: to cave-in   *ant: to overcome*

Exercise I — Words in Context

From the words below, supply the words needed to complete the sentences.

engrossed	improvise	shun	subterranean	profound

A.   The group of moles was wary. Because of the traps they had to _____ all their usual _____ mazes of tunnels.

B.   Since Albert hadn't studied, he tried to _____ an answer. _____ in his own reply, he didn't notice the rest of the class smirking at what he thought were _____ comments.

From the words below, supply the words needed to complete the sentences.

regatta	rail	prodigy	viable	impunity

C.   Until they are caught, most criminals think they can commit their crimes with complete _____.

D.   The only _____ entry left in the _____ was a sleek, two-masted sailboat.

E.   The foreman of the plant would frequently _____ for hours at his workers' sloppiness.

F.   When James performed on the piano at age eight, the critics called him a _____.

From the words below, supply the words needed to complete the sentences.

aspirant	flamboyant	opportune	indigent	succumbed

G.   No one came to visit the sickly, _____ man in the hospital. When he finally _____ to cancer, he died alone.

H.   The general decided that the most _____ time to launch an invasion was at dawn.

I.   The wrestler looked _____ in his red and gold robes.

J.   Every _____ to win an Olympic Medal must train rigorously for years.

Exercise II—Analogies //

Complete the analogy by choosing the most appropriate word.

1. hero : bravery ::
   A. gunfighter : quickness
   B. villain : victim
   C. sailor : seasickness
   D. president : election

2. deception : falsehood ::
   A. robbery : murder
   B. choice : selection
   C. behavior : detention
   D. qualify : attribute

3. thoroughbred : horse ::
   A. mink : fox
   B. mast : ship
   C. orca : whale
   D. matador : bull

Exercise III—Roots, Prefixes, and Suffixes //

You have now gone through 16 lessons which included roots, prefixes, and suffixes. In order to see how well you have studied and understood those word parts, here is a list of all of them from this book. See if you can make up some actual and some nonsense words, using combinations of the prefixes, roots, and suffixes; across from each new word YOU make up, write out a definition. We have done four for you.

Prefixes	Roots	Suffixes
in	tech	able
un	vert	ible
dis	contra	ism
trans	terr	ary
hypo	cycl	ic
hyper	hydro	ous
pre	hemo	phobia
intra	claustro	phile
inter	bibl	
uni	arach	
bi	anglo	
tri	viv	
quad		
quint		
sex		
sep		
oct		
nona		
dec		

intechphobia   -   not fearing skills
biterrism   -   related to two lands
cyclous   -   like a circle
incontrovertible   -   not able to be turned against

1. _____ - _____
2. _____ - _____
3. _____ - _____
4. _____ - _____
5. _____ - _____
6. _____ - _____

71

7. _____ - _____
8. _____ - _____
9. _____ - _____
10. _____ - _____

Exercise IV—Reading Comprehension

Read the selection and answer the questions.

One nuclear agency, headed by William Martin of the U.S., is currently working on a new project, called Agent Defeat Weapons Concept Exploration. The end result is to destroy stockpiles of an enemy's biological or chemical weapons, while not also killing people, leaving soldiers without the means to continue to wage war. This would be the first truly "new" weapon since the Atomic Bomb.

Interviews have revealed that the development has been daunting and has been underway in complete secrecy. Previously our apparent enemy would have been the Soviet Union; now, however, an all-out nuclear war is less likely and America's 65,000 nuclear weapons would be essentially useless against small groups of terrorists. Consequently, a new approach is necessary.

Many methods have been explored by the scientists working on the project, including lasers, vibrating bombs, sticky gels, foams, and air-sprayed acids. Each new solution posed new problems. For example, sticky gels could have been bombed on enemies' bunkers, preventing soldiers from entering. That solution was quickly abandoned, because of countermeasures to render the gel useless, regardless of its initial stickiness. Ozone was considered, also, but because it cannot be stored for a long while, it, too, was eliminated from consideration as a solution.

Finally, six concepts were given approval for final testing, as long as they could meet three criteria: cost, effectiveness, and ability to counter a wide array of chemical and biological weapons. After testing, only the vibrating bomb, which produces extremely low-level sounds, below human ability to hear, seems to work well enough to merit further consideration. The sounds produced break down chemicals, such as gases, and diseases, such as anthrax, into harmless particles.

The major problem plaguing the entire project, though, seems to be that it is entirely dependent on a potential enemy not improving its weapons-protection capabilities, and that is one aspect scientists cannot predict accurately.

1. The best title for this article would be
   A. New Weapons Under Development.
   B. Destroying Enemies.
   C. Vibrating Bomb Works Well.
   D. Project to Kill Weapons, Save Lives.
   E. Space-Age Weapons.

2. According to the article,
   A. the vibrating bomb works best.
   B. many problems exist in each solution.
   C. cost is a factor in determining which weapons to develop.
   D. America had prepared to fight a nuclear war in the past.
   E. All the above are correct.

3. The three elements necessary for approval in the final phase are: (paragraph 4)
   A. potential, cost, and range.
   B. effectiveness, money, and safety.
   C. what's destroyed, difficulty to make, amount of money necessary.
   D. ability to not kill people, ease of use, and cost.
   E. None of the above is correct.

4. What is one difference between how war was prepared for previously and the new developments?
   A. Previous wars have been nuclear.
   B. Cities were the main targets.
   C. Only soldiers were destroyed.
   D. Attempts are being made to ruin an enemy's desire to fight.
   E. The enemy may be a group, not a nation.